Ryd

MW00399650

TABLE OF CONTENTS

Outline of Jeremiah

I. Oracles against Judah and Jerusalem (Chapters 1–25)
    A. Oracles from the time of Josiah (Chapters 1–6)
        1. Jeremiah's call (Chapter 1)
        2. Israel's unfaithfulness (Chapters 2–3)
        3. The foe from the north (Chapter 4)
        4. Israel's punishment (Chapters 5–6)
    B. Oracles from the time of Jehoiakim (Chapters 7–20)
        1. Jeremiah's Temple sermon (Chapter 7)
        2. Oracles concerning Judah (Chapters 8–10)
        3. Jeremiah's laments (Chapters 11–20)
    C. Oracles from the time of Zedekiah (Chapters 21-25)
    D. Oracles concerning Judah and Ephraim (Chapters 28–35)

II. The memoirs of Baruch (Chapters 26–45)
    A. Events and prophecies (Chapters 26–35)
        1. Temple sermon (Chapter 26)
        2. Prophecy concerning Babylon (Chapters 27–28)
        3. Jeremiah's letters to Babylon (Chapter 29)
        4. The Book of Consolation (Chapters 30–31)
        5. Miscellaneous events and oracles (Chapters 32–35)
    B. Trials and sufferings of Jeremiah (Chapters 36–45)
        1. Jeremiah, Jehoiakim, and Zedekiah (Chapters 36-38)
        2. The fall of Jerusalem (Chapters 39–41)
        3. Jeremiah in Egypt (Chapters 42–45)

III. Oracles against foreign nations (Chapters 46–51)
    A. Oracle against Egypt (Chapter 46)
    B. Oracle against the Philistines (Chapter 47)
    C. Oracle against Moab (Chapter 48)
    D. Oracle against Edom (Chapter 49)
    E. Oracles against Babylon (Chapters 50–51)

IV. Historical appendix (Chapter 52)

Introduction to Jeremiah: To Sort Through a Life

Have you ever come across, in an attic or a closet, a box of mementos carefully saved by a relative or friend? If you have, you know the mixed emotions such a discovery can bring. First, perhaps, you feel an amused, loving sort of disgust. ("What *is* all this junk, and why isn't it in some sort of order instead of just being tossed into a box?") Then, you become curious about individual items. ("When do you suppose she wore that corsage?") Finally, you feel wonder and delight as you find yourself gaining new insight into a dear one's personality. ("I never realized how much those silly poems meant to him!")

Reading the Book of Jeremiah is a lot like sorting through a box of mementos. The book is a disorderly (though not completely haphazard) collection of literature relating to one of Israel's greatest prophets. In the Book of Jeremiah, you will find a letter, sermons, short prophetic utterances, snatches of biographical information, the reminiscences of friends, and prayers that reflect Jeremiah's most intimate struggles. You will find pedestrian prose and magnificent poetry, some by the prophet himself, some by others. This book is very personal and will show you, by bits and pieces, the heart of a man who loved, served, and wrestled with God.

This book is also a political-historical book. Jeremiah was closely involved with Israel's national policies during a time of major political upheaval. He spoke with kings and ambassadors. He tried to explain God's purposes and desires in the midst of international turmoil. His life and words were directly related to national and world events.

To understand mementos whose owner had been deeply involved in politics, you would probably need to know something about the political events of the time. Many of Jeremiah's words make sense only in light of the international situation he was addressing. Here is a brief sketch of what was happening.

At the time of Jeremiah's birth, Assyria controlled a vast Middle Eastern empire that extended from Asia Minor into Egypt. Gradually, however, that empire weakened. Under Josiah, Judah broke away. A religious reform accompanied this move toward independence. But the reform soon met with resistance among its foes and misinterpretation among its friends. Meanwhile, in Babylonia another world power was rising. The Egyptians were determined to stop that power before it went too far. As the new empire pushed relentlessly southward, Judah was embroiled in a complex religious and political crisis. This crisis threatened Judah's very existence and reshaped its understanding of what it meant to be God's chosen people.

The Jeremiah mementos show us how one prophet tried to bring God's word to the people at this pivotal point in their national and religious history. Understanding the man will be easier if you can keep in mind the situation behind these bits and pieces. To help you keep things in historical perspective, we have provided a chart (pages 6–7) showing major events reflected in the book.

Now you have some tools for understanding. The Jeremiah collection is available. So let's open it up and see what's inside!

Historical Times at the Time of Jeremiah

Kings of Judah	Alliances	Political Events	Events in Jeremiah's Life
Manasseh 687–642 B.C.	Assyria		6? Jeremiah born
Amon 642–640	Assyria		
Josiah 640–609	Babylonia	627 Death of strong Assyrian king, Asshurbanipal 626 Babylonia rebels against Assyria 622 Discovery of Deuteronomic scroll 612 Nineveh, capital of Assyria, falls	627 Jeremiah's call
Jehoahaz 609	Babylonia	609 Battle of Megiddo, Josiah killed by Egyptians	609? Temple sermon; Jeremiah narrowly escapes death
Jehoiakim 609–598	Egypt	605 Battle of Carchemish, Babylonia defeats Egypt and establishes control over Assyrian empire	Dictates scroll that is promptly burned by Jehoiakim

JEREMIAH AND LAMENTATIONS

Ruler	Policy	Events	Jeremiah
Jehoiachin 598		598 Jehoiakim refuses tribute to Babylonia, then dies; siege of Jerusalem; Jehoiachin surrenders; first deportation	Preaches and is put in stocks by Pashhur; brings Rechabites into Temple
Zedekiah 598–587	Vacillates between Babylonia and Egypt	594 Ambassadors meet to plot revolt 589 Judah rebels, Babylonians besiege Jerusalem 588 Egyptian force distracts Babylonians, lifting the siege temporarily	594 Wears yoke to symbolize submission to Babylonia, has confrontation with Hananiah; writes letter to exiles 588 Attempts to visit Anathoth, is arrested and imprisoned, purchases field
Gedaliah (governor) 587	Babylonia	587 Jerusalem destroyed, many citizens carried into exile 5?? Gedaliah assassinated	587 Chooses to stay in Judah 500 Forcibly taken to Egypt where he eventually dies

Stand up and say to them
whatever I command you (1:17).

1

Stand Up and Speak

Jeremiah 1–3

DIMENSION ONE:
WHAT DOES THE BIBLE SAY?

Answer these questions by reading Jeremiah 1

1. Where is Jeremiah's hometown? (1:1)

2. What is his family's profession? (1:1)

3. When does the word of the Lord come? (1:2-3)

4. Who is speaking in verse 4? in verse 5? in verse 6?

5. When did God appoint Jeremiah as prophet? (1:5)

6. When Jeremiah recognizes God's call, how does he respond? (1:6)

7. What reassurance does God offer? (1:8)

8. What two items does God show Jeremiah, and what do they mean? (1:11-16)

9. With whom will Jeremiah come in conflict? (1:18-19)

10. What promise does God make? (1:19)

Answer these questions by reading Jeremiah 2

11. What has characterized Israel's past relationship with God? (2:2)

12. How has the relationship changed? (2:4-8)

13. Picturesque language compares God with the popular idols. Which image describes God? Which describes the idols? (2:13)

14. What misfortune has Israel experienced, and why?
    (2:14-19)

15. What images describe Israel's sinful nature? (2:20-37)

16. Of what additional sin is Israel guilty? (2:34)

Answer these questions by reading Jeremiah 3

17. Judah and Israel are compared to two sisters. Which sister
    has the greater guilt? (3:6-11)

18. How should the people respond when confronted with
    their sins? (3:21-23)

DIMENSION TWO:
WHAT DOES THE BIBLE MEAN?

In these first three chapters we meet Jeremiah, learn a few
basic facts about his life, then plunge directly into some of his
earliest personal experiences with God. We then encounter
his later personal experiences with God. Finally, we encounter
a collection of his early messages.

❏ *Jeremiah 1.* The book opens with an editorial note on Jeremiah and his prophecies. The remainder of the chapter is the
prophet's own account of his call and early visions.

❏ *Jeremiah 1:1-3.* This introduction probably opened an early
collection of Jeremiah's prophecies. Note that its final date is

the capture of Jerusalem in 587 B.C. We know from Chapters 41–44, however, that Jeremiah continued to prophesy for an indefinite time after the city's fall.

Anathoth is a village about two miles northeast of Jerusalem.

❑ *Jeremiah 1:4-10.* Here Jeremiah describes his call. In this brief conversation we can feel keenly his sense of personal destiny, of responsibility, and of impending danger.

❑ *Jeremiah 1:11-16.* This account of two prophetic experiences breaks into Jeremiah's description of his call. The incidents may have occurred in connection with his call, or they may have happened somewhat later.

Jeremiah's first bit of prophetic insight is precipitated by a branch or stick from an almond tree. The Hebrew word for *almond* is *saqed*. It suggested to Jeremiah a similar word, *soqed*, which means *watching*. Thus the prophet becomes aware of God's determination, or watching, to see the divine intentions fulfilled.

The second experience involves a boiling pot. The pot is not sitting firmly on the fire but is tilted toward the south. If it overflows, the contents will spill out on the south side. Seeing this pot, Jeremiah realizes that an unstable situation to the north is about to boil over. It will pour out onto Judah, giving the nation a scalding. All this is no accident, either. God is punishing Judah for Judah's repeated sinfulness.

❑ *Jeremiah 1:17-19.* In these three verses God again promises to remain with Jeremiah, strengthening and protecting him.

❑ *Jeremiah 2.* Here we begin a series of early oracles or messages. All these oracles focus on the problems of faithlessness and idolatry. They probably come from early in the reign of Josiah before the king's reform movement had taken hold. Or they might come from the time of Josiah's son Jehoiakim, who allowed his father's reform to lapse. The people have raced after other gods, and we can hear in Jeremiah's words the anger and disgust he feels at their faithlessness. We hear, too, a desperate word of warning: Turn back! You are bringing destruction upon yourselves by forsaking your God!

❑ *Jeremiah 2:5.* The word translated here as *worthless* is sometimes translated as *delusion*. The word in Hebrew plays upon the name *Baal*, the Canaanite fertility god. By using this particular word, Jeremiah subtly underlines Baal's unreality and impotence.

❑ *Jeremiah 2:10.* This verse mentions Cyprus (or Kittim) and Kedar. Kedar is a desert area east of Palestine. Cyprus is an island in the Mediterranean. The verse simply means "Look from east to west and see if you can find anything like this."

❑ *Jeremiah 2:16-19.* Jeremiah points out Israel's subjugation and insists that faithlessness to God has brought it about. Memphis and Tahpanhes are two Egyptian cities. This passage, then, comes from a time after Josiah's defeat and Israel's subordination to Egypt.

❑ *Jeremiah 2:20-28.* Next we find a series of metaphors describing the depravity and the ultimate foolishness of Israel's sin. These verses provide an excellent example of the imaginative, poetic, and devastatingly precise mind of Jeremiah.

The high hills and spreading trees of verse 20 refer to pagan religious practices. The fertility cults worshiped on hilltops and regarded trees as sacred objects.

The valley of verse 23 is probably the valley of Hinnom outside Jerusalem. This valley is famous as the scene of orgies and child sacrifice in the name of Baal.

❑ *Jeremiah 2:29-37.* The accusation against Israel continues. Note that verses 36-37 suggest a time when Israel is looking toward Egypt for support.

❑ *Jeremiah 3.* This chapter continues the denunciation of Israel's idolatry. Here, however, Jeremiah concentrates on a single image, that of Israel as a promiscuous woman.

❑ *Jeremiah 3:14.* Zion was originally the name of David's fortified hill at Jerusalem. Later the name was extended to the Temple area. Eventually the name *Zion* came to stand for the entire city of Jerusalem and/or the people who lived there. In the books of Jeremiah and Lamentations, Zion usually has this broader meaning.

But the word *Zion* is more than a geographical place name. The word carries with it a special religious connotation. Zion is that sacred spot (temple or city) where God's presence touches the earth. When persons come to Zion, they are in fact coming into the presence of God.

❑ *Jeremiah 3:16-18.* This passage comes from a much later time, since it assumes the exile of both Israel and Judah from their homeland. (Israel was exiled in 721 B.C., and Judah was exiled in 587 B.C.) Verse 16 mentions "the ark of the covenant of the LORD." The sacred ark was taken from the Temple by the Babylonians in 587 B.C.

❑ *Jeremiah 3:21-25.* The final five verses of Chapter 3 are a plea for repentance and a model of the response God wants from the people. In these verses, the image is no longer female. The people are now compared to disloyal, ungrateful sons, with God as the grieving father.

DIMENSION THREE:
WHAT DOES THE BIBLE MEAN TO ME?

Two topics dominate this session's biblical material: the call to speak for God and the problem of idolatry. Let's consider now their meaning for us.

Jeremiah 2:4-13—The Problem of Idolatry

You probably know persons who place their faith somewhere other than in God. Where are they placing their hopes? Do we as a nation look elsewhere for help? Do you personally look for security and satisfaction somewhere else? If so, where?

Jeremiah says that idolatry makes us look foolish and causes us to become as worthless as the idols we worship. Do our contemporary idols make us act foolishly? If so, how? How can we grow worthless by placing our faith in something less than God? Give examples to support your answer.

Jeremiah 1:4-11—The Call to Speak for God

These verses describe Jeremiah's call to be a prophet. What kind of person does it take to be a prophet?

Is everyone called to speak for God or only select persons? Could you be called? If so, how would you know that you had been called?

If you were called to be a prophet, how might you or your church speak the word of God in today's idolatrous world? Would your actions involve some risk? If so, what might happen if you accepted the risk?

Food for Thought

When will you see idolatry or hear the call of God? Try to remain alert to these possibilities in the coming week. You may be surprised at the number of such experiences you have!

Oh, my anguish, my anguish!
I writhe in pain. . . .
For I have heard the sound of the trumpet;
I have heard the battle cry (4:19).

2

I See a Bitter End

Jeremiah 4–6

DIMENSION ONE:
WHAT DOES THE BIBLE SAY?

Answer these questions by reading Jeremiah 4

1. What does God want the people to do? (4:1)

2. What punishment is God planning for Judah? (4:6-7)

3. What has brought on this disaster? (4:17-18)

4. How does Jeremiah feel when he thinks about the impending catastrophe? (4:19)

5. Judah is pictured as a prostitute. What is the prostitute looking for, and what will she get instead? (4:30-31)

Answer these questions by reading Jeremiah 5

6. What task does God assign Jeremiah, and why? (5:1)

7. What kind of people does Jeremiah find? (5:2)

8. What sins does Jeremiah condemn? (5:7-8)

9. What is Jeremiah's assignment? (5:10)

10. What attitude has angered God? (5:12)

11. What punishment will the prophets receive? (5:13)

12. What image describes Jeremiah's task? (5:14)

13. How will Judah be destroyed? (5:15-17)

14. How does Jeremiah speak of the people? (5:23)

Answer these questions by reading Jeremiah 6

15. What does God tell Jeremiah to do? (6:9)

16. What does Jeremiah expect to find? (6:10)

17. How does this situation make Jeremiah feel? (6:11)

18. Of what other sins does Jeremiah accuse the people? (6:13)

19. How does God respond to the people's offerings and sacrifices? Why? (6:19-20)

20. What is Jeremiah's task in verse 27?

DIMENSION TWO:
WHAT DOES THE BIBLE MEAN?

In this session we see Jeremiah recognizing both the depth of his people's sin and the magnitude of disaster they are courting. The short, varied pieces in these chapters reflect Jeremiah's horror at the coming destruction, his efforts to avert it by warning the people, and his awareness of his own complex role as God's agent and spokesperson. The passages are not easy to date. Most are later than those we studied in

Lesson 1. They might fit in anywhere from late in Josiah's reign to the approach of Nebuchadnezzar in 598 B.C.

❑ *Jeremiah 4.* This chapter opens with God's call for Judah's return. A clear choice is offered. The people can either come back to the Lord and receive blessing or stay as they are and suffer God's wrath. The remaining portions of this chapter include several vivid descriptions of the coming destruction and a glimpse of what it means to the prophet personally.

❑ *Jeremiah 4:1-4.* Notice that what God asks here is somewhat more complex than the demands we found in Chapters 1–3. There, the most obvious problem was idolatry; and rejection of idols was a major goal. Now a religious reform has taken place. Idolatry is outlawed, but sin still abounds. Jeremiah recognizes that what is really needed is a cleansing of the heart, inward dedication, and ethical behavior. Therefore, verse 3 suggests cultivating and weeding out the heart. Circumcision (verse 4) is an act of dedication, but here it is clearly dedication of the heart that God really wants.

❑ *Jeremiah 4:6-7.* "Disaster from the north" probably refers to the rising power of Babylonia. Nebuchadnezzar could be expected to move first westward to conquer Assyria, then turn southward to Judah. However, it is possible that Jeremiah had in mind one of several earlier invaders.

❑ *Jeremiah 4:10.* This remark shows Jeremiah's frustration. He realizes that the abolition of idolatry and the words of corrupt prophets had lulled the people into a false security. Since they have fulfilled the surface requirements of the law, they believe they have done all that is needed. Jeremiah may be angry that this misunderstanding has come through religious, and presumably God-inspired, channels.

❑ *Jeremiah 4:15.* Dan is the northernmost territory of Palestine. Dan is also the first area to see an attack from the north. Mount Ephraim (or "the hills of Ephraim") would be farther south, just a few miles north of Jerusalem.

❑ *Jeremiah 4:19-22.* Here we sense the depth of pain Jeremiah feels as he contemplates his people's foolishness and their eventual suffering.

❏ *Jeremiah 4:23-26.* This picture of destruction is cosmic, a sort of reverse Creation.

❏ *Jeremiah 4:27.* The final note, "I will not destroy it completely," is probably a later addition. The comment reflects Jeremiah's or an editor's knowledge that the Babylonian conquest did not completely destroy Palestine.

❏ *Jeremiah 4:30-31.* As in Chapters 2 and 3, Jeremiah compares Judah to a harlot. This time he particularly emphasizes the sordid end a prostitute may meet. In Judah's case the lovers are apparently other nations (Egypt or Assyria, for example) from whom she is trying to obtain favors at the cost of her religious integrity.

❏ *Jeremiah 5.* The oracles in Chapter 5 emphasize the tragic conflict between God's desire to pardon Judah and the people's persistence in sin. Jeremiah stands in the middle of that conflict.

❏ *Jeremiah 5:1-5.* Here we see two facets of Jeremiah's role as an intermediary between God and the people. First he works with God trying to find an upright man. Jeremiah is looking for one whose goodness might serve as a reason to spare the entire group. When Jeremiah can find none among the common people, he takes on the role of intercessor. He makes excuses to God and suggests that, given a little more time, he will surely find someone; but to his disappointment, even the nation's leaders have turned away. Like oxen who have broken their yokes, they have escaped both the owner's demands and his protection. The entire passage shows clearly how much both God and the prophet want to save the people, not punish them.

❏ *Jeremiah 5:10-17.* These verses illustrate another facet of Jeremiah's task. He is to serve as an agent of destruction. Or at least he is to administer a thorough pruning. He is not, of course, to go on a rampage through the city. But the word of a Hebrew prophet carries the power of God. Jeremiah's preaching will call forth the punishment God intends.

❏ *Jeremiah 5:18-19.* This note is a later addition that reflects upon the Exile in Babylon.

❏ *Jeremiah 5:20-31.* The sins mentioned here involve injustice, lack of concern for the poor, failure to recognize God's sovereignty, and a watered-down Yahwism. Although it may still be present, idolatry is no longer the central issue.

❑ *Jeremiah 6.* This chapter contains several more of Jeremiah's warnings. As before, he points out the people's sin and describes the desolation to come. But his prophetic task goes beyond giving mere warnings. Jeremiah is also expected to test, to judge, to search out any righteous who remain, and to try to remove corrupt elements from within the nation.

❑ *Jeremiah 6:9.* Jeremiah here is told to pick through the leavings to see if anything worthwhile in Judah has been missed. God is still reluctant to condemn the entire nation when a few righteous persons may remain.

❑ *Jeremiah 6:27-30.* Jeremiah is pictured here as an assayer, a tester, and a refiner of metal. In ancient times, lead was used to separate alloys from silver. In these verses, however, the silver (Judah) is so impure that the lead cannot absorb all the alloys. Jeremiah has found his people hopelessly corrupt.

DIMENSION THREE:
WHAT DOES THE BIBLE MEAN TO ME?

Jeremiah 4:19-22—Judgment on the People

Have you ever watched someone you loved making a very big mistake? Perhaps a friend was consciously choosing an option that you knew to be wrong. Or perhaps a relative was drifting unconsciously into a grief-laden lifestyle. How did this situation make you feel?

Jeremiah saw his prophetic role as one of testing, judging, warning, and administering punishment. Matthew 7:1-5, however, warns us, "Do not judge, or you too will be judged." What do you think? Are we to judge, warn, and perhaps even punish those we see going wrong? Or are we to monitor and discipline ourselves only?

Jeremiah 5:7-9—Why Should I Forgive You?

Jeremiah apparently started off with high hopes for saving his people. Later his hopes declined. Do you see this as a normal pattern or simply as an individual experience? Do you find less or more good in people now than you did ten years ago?

Jeremiah 5:30-31
The Responsibility of Religious Leaders

In these verses Jeremiah expresses special concern that religious leaders have capitulated to the people's desire for a reassuring, comfortable religion. In doing so, these priests and prophets have ignored the authentic word of God. How do you feel about pastors who do not speak out against specific sins? Are they more blameworthy than the congregations they lead? Does apathy or corruption by clergy upset you more than similar sins committed by a layperson? Why or why not?

So far we have been talking primarily about individual errors. But Jeremiah was not. He was speaking of a great national trend, a social phenomenon involving everyone. What evidence can you see of national sin today? Could such sin lead the United States to disaster? If so, how?

If our nation were heading toward sin-induced disaster, should anything be done? If so, what should be done? By whom?

Food for Thought

We have talked a lot in this session about recognizing and responding to the errors around us. In the coming week, try to notice especially those times when you become aware of individuals or groups making wrong choices. Then think through carefully and prayerfully what God expects of you within those situations. Remember: Jeremiah's job took many forms; yours probably will, too.

*Oh, that I had in the desert
a lodging place for travelers,
so that I might leave my people
and go away from them (9:2).*

3

I Despise Them, God
Jeremiah 7–11

DIMENSION ONE:
WHAT DOES THE BIBLE SAY?

Answer these questions by reading Jeremiah 7

1. Where does God send Jeremiah to proclaim his word?
   (7:2)

2. What deceptive idea (or words) does Jeremiah warn
   against? (7:3-4)

3. What does God really want the people to do? (7:5-7)

4. What is God planning to do to his house, and why?
   (7:12-14)

5. What unusual command does God give Jeremiah, and why? (7:16-20)

6. From the time he brought them out of Egypt, God has expected certain kinds of behavior from the people. What has been the essential covenant command? What practices are not central to the original covenant? (7:21-23)

7. Jeremiah is to remind the people of their covenant responsibility. But what is their likely response? (7:27-28)

Answer these questions by reading Jeremiah 8

8. How does God feel the people are behaving? (8:4-7)

9. As the people suffer, what does Jeremiah feel? (8:18-21)

10. What hope does Jeremiah have? (8:22)

Answer these questions by reading Jeremiah 9

11. What two conflicting feelings does Jeremiah have toward the people? (9:1-2)

12. What will Judah be like after God's punishment? (9:10-11)

13. Where does the wise man find satisfaction and worth? (9:23-24)

14. Why is Israel listed among those who are "circumcised only in the flesh . . . uncircumcised in heart"? (9:25-26)

Answer these questions by reading Jeremiah 10

15. What is the opening poem's main point? (10:5, 15-16)

16. What personal prayer does Jeremiah pray? (10:23-24)

Answer these questions by reading Jeremiah 11

17. Where will Judah vainly seek help in time of trouble? (11:12, 15)

18. What plot has been laid against Jeremiah? (11:19-21)

19. What does Jeremiah pray for? (11:20)

20. Why does Jeremiah feel justified in asking for this? (11:20)

21. What punishment does Jeremiah anticipate for these men? (11:22-23)

DIMENSION TWO:
WHAT DOES THE BIBLE MEAN?

Chapters 7–11 contain portions of Jeremiah's Temple Sermon. They also contain miscellaneous speeches, poems, prayers, and personal notes. Within these chapters we see again Jeremiah's deep concern for his people, but we also discover his anger and vindictiveness.

❏ *Jeremiah 7.* Chapter 7 begins with Jeremiah's call to preach a public sermon in the Temple gate. The incident probably occurred during Jehoiakim's reign. At that time, Josiah's religious reform had gone stale. Verses 3-15 seem to contain the gist of this "Temple Sermon." And a shocking sermon it was, condemning standard religious ideas as worthless and denouncing common practice as faithless hypocrisy! The remaining verses in the chapter are a collection of similar materials decrying the people's sin and warning of the punishment it has earned them. The people have been worshiping in cultic places and using cultic practices.

❏ *Jeremiah 7:12.* Shiloh, about eighteen miles north of Jerusalem, was the site of an important early shrine. The city was destroyed, apparently by the Philistines, around 1500 B.C.

❏ *Jeremiah 7:18.* The Queen of Heaven was a popular Assyrian goddess.

❏ *Jeremiah 8–10.* These chapters contain miscellaneous oracles, most of which point out the people's sin and the punishment God intends. In the final verses of Chapter 8, however, we find a personal cry of anguish over the suffering to come. In Jeremiah 9:1-2, we glimpse some of the conflicting feelings the prophet holds toward his people.

❏ *Jeremiah 8:16.* Dan was the northernmost territory of Israel.

❏ *Jeremiah 8:22.* Gilead was a city noted for its medicinal products. The "balm of Gilead" was an aromatic, antiseptic, soothing ointment exported from Gilead.

❏ *Jeremiah 9:25-26.* Circumcision signified Israel's dedication to God. Arabs and Egyptians also practiced physical circumcision, but they were not God's people in the way that Israel was intended to be.

Cutting the corners of the hair (See the text note in the NIV—"shaven temples" in the NRSV.) was an Arabian religious practice.

❏ *Jeremiah 10:1-16.* This poem is probably a later editorial addition to Jeremiah. The author of this poem shares Jeremiah's disdain for idols. The poem is almost certainly exilic or later and shows many similarities to the speeches of Second Isaiah.

❏ *Jeremiah 10:9.* Tarshish was located in Spain or Sardinia. The location of Uphaz is unknown.

❏ *Jeremiah 10:25.* This quote from Psalm 79:6-7 is also probably an editorial addition.

❏ *Jeremiah 11.* Chapter 11 begins with additional sermons on God's fundamental covenant demands. But in verses 18-23 we learn of a dramatic incident in Jeremiah's personal life. Threatened by a plot to murder him, the prophet unleashes his anger in a vindictive prayer against his enemies.

DIMENSION THREE:
WHAT DOES THE BIBLE MEAN TO ME?

In this session we have discovered two more aspects of Jeremiah's complex personality: (1) He sometimes held quite ambivalent feelings toward the people he was trying so hard to save, and (2) when personally threatened, he could lash out in bitter vindictiveness. Now in this portion of the lesson let's try relating Jeremiah's experiences to our own.

Jeremiah 9:1-2—Those Ambivalent Feelings

Read Jeremiah 9:1-2 again. Have you ever had mixed feelings like these toward someone you were trying to help? If so, what brought on those feelings?

Is it wrong to wish to escape from someone who needs your help? Can you give some examples of times when you have wanted to escape from someone needing your help? Is it wrong to carry out that escape wish? Would your answer be the same in every circumstance?

Jeremiah 11:19-23—The Desire for Revenge

Now turn to Jeremiah 11:19-20. How does Jeremiah feel here? How would you express these feelings? (Try to put Jeremiah's response into your own words.)

Jeremiah's reaction was a common one, but compare it with Jesus' response in Luke 23:33-34. Which prayer is more mature? Which is harder to pray? Which is more satisfying?

Read Jeremiah 11:21-23. Might Jeremiah's own vindictiveness have colored his perception of God's will here? Could your own emotions affect your understanding of God's will? Can you imagine any other answer God might give to a prayer like Jeremiah's?

What can you do when you find yourself reacting vindictively? Does it surprise you that someone as spiritually mature as Jeremiah could display the traits we have discovered in this session? Does it surprise you to find character flaws in contemporary religious leaders?

What could you say to a friend who felt unworthy to serve in a church leadership role because of some personal imperfection? Have you yourself ever felt this way? If so, how did you solve the dilemma?

Food for Thought

Sometime in the days ahead you may experience some negative feelings toward others. You may inwardly churn with vindictiveness or with the impulse to escape from those you love. What will you do? Spend some time this week planning the kind of response you would most like to make when these events arise.

Why is my pain unending
and my wound grievous and incurable? (15:18).

4

Why, God, Why?

Jeremiah 12–15

DIMENSION ONE:
WHAT DOES THE BIBLE SAY?

Answer these questions by reading Jeremiah 12

1. What complaint or question does Jeremiah bring before
   God? (12:1)

2. What does Jeremiah want God to do to the wicked? (12:3)

3. How does God respond to Jeremiah's question? (12:5)

4. Why has evil come upon God's people? (12:13)

Answer these questions by reading Jeremiah 13

5. What does God command Jeremiah to do, and what do
   these actions signify? (13:1-11)

6. What popular saying does Jeremiah use, and what special meaning does he draw from it? (13:12-14)

7. What does Jeremiah plead with the people to do? (13:16)

8. Why is Judah overrun and facing exile? (13:22)

9. How great are Judah's chances of learning to do good? (13:23)

Answer these questions by reading Jeremiah 14

10. What disaster has come upon Judah? (14:1-6)

11. After confessing their sins, what questions do the people ask? (14:7-9)

12. What answer do they receive? (14:10)

13. What disturbs Jeremiah about Judah's religious leaders? (14:18)

14. What questions open Judah's prayer? (14:19)

15. What have the people expected but not received? (14:19)

16. Do the people acknowledge any responsibility for the evil that has come upon them? (14:20)

17. According to the people, why should God not despise them? (14:21)

Answer these questions by reading Jeremiah 15

18. How does God respond to this prayer? (15:1)

19. How does Jeremiah feel, and why? (15:10)

20. Why does Jeremiah complain that he should not be so mistreated by the people? (15:10)

21. What sacrifices has Jeremiah made in order to serve God faithfully? (15:15-18)

22. What angry questions does Jeremiah ask God? (15:18)

23. How does God answer Jeremiah? (15:19)

24. What promise does God give? (15:20)

DIMENSION TWO:
WHAT DOES THE BIBLE MEAN?

Chapters 12–15 contain many small, disconnected pieces. Prayers, oracles, stray bits from later writers, an acted-out prophecy, and poems expressing Jeremiah's own inner struggles are included. Evidences of suffering permeate these pieces. And with the suffering come some agonizing questions about God's relationship to the people.

❑ *Jeremiah 12.* In this chapter we learn of a question that greatly troubles Jeremiah. From there we turn to a poem expressing God's deep anger with Judah. A later passage that speaks of God's anger toward Israel's neighbors has been added after the poem.

❑ *Jeremiah 12:1-3.* Here Jeremiah confronts a question that threatens to undermine his faith: Why does a righteous God allow the wicked to prosper? Why does God not strike them down? Doesn't God see? Doesn't God care? Why is God not doing something? For a prophet who has spent his life preaching about the inevitable doom of sinners, this is an agonizing question indeed.

❑ *Jeremiah 12:4.* This verse appears to be out of place. It interrupts the conversational flow between 12:3 and 12:5.

❑ *Jeremiah 12:5-6.* God's answer is really no answer at all. It is a mildly reproachful reminder that Jeremiah will have to face tougher questions than this before he is finished.

❏ *Jeremiah 12:7.* "House" could mean either the Temple or the nation. The word *inheritance* refers to the land of Israel or to the people.

❏ *Jeremiah 12:9.* The speckled bird is a bird of brightly colored plumage, one that other birds might attack in jealousy.

❏ *Jeremiah 12:14-17.* This prose addition offers hope for conversion of Israel's enemies. This idea came into prominence only after the Exile.

❏ *Jeremiah 13.* In this chapter Jeremiah uses a dramatic series of actions, a popular proverb, and impassioned pleading in his efforts to alert his people to the consequences of sin.

❏ *Jeremiah 13:1-11.* In this dramatic public demonstration, Jeremiah uses a "linen belt" to illustrate the ruin that is coming at the hands of the Babylonians. This "belt" is really a skirtlike undergarment reaching from the hips to about halfway down the thighs.

The Euphrates was a major Babylonian river. (See the footnote for verse 4.)

❏ *Jeremiah 13:12-14.* "Every wineskin should be filled with wine" was apparently a common saying. The word *wineskin* carries a double meaning. It refers to both the container and the drinkers themselves. But Jeremiah adds a new twist to the saying. He suggests that the people will behave like shameful, disgusting drunks. They will lose their ability to think straight. Then God will smash them like so many jars.

❏ *Jeremiah 13:18.* The king mentioned here is probably the young Jehoiachin, who reigned only three months before surrendering to the Babylonians in 597 B.C.

❏ *Jeremiah 13:19.* The Negev is a district in the southern part of Judah. Town gates there were shut tight against the Babylonian attackers.

❏ *Jeremiah 14.* In this chapter Jeremiah addresses several disaster situations. His words show us the people's dismay at their misfortune, God's fierce determination to continue the punishment, and the prophet's own concern over the deplorable state of his nation.

❏ *Jeremiah 15.* The first part of this chapter speaks of Judah's sin, God's wrath, and the inevitability of disaster. But in verse 10 we move into a very different matter. Here Jeremiah stands before God screaming in anger at the personal pain he must bear. He has faithfully carried out God's commands. He has risked his life, his reputation, and certainly his comfort and happiness to serve the Lord. And what is his reward? He is laughed at, persecuted, lonely, and utterly miserable. So Jeremiah must face one of the toughest questions of his life: Can I really trust God, or is it all a cruel cosmic joke? And God's answer is more of a challenge than an explanation.

❑ *Jeremiah 15:1-4.* Both Moses and Samuel were noted for their efforts at intercession. And both were powerful religious figures who might be supposed to have some extra influence with God.

Verse 4 is an addition that blames the people's suffering on the idolatries of Manasseh.

❑ *Jeremiah 15:12.* The words *iron* and *bronze* apparently refer to the stubborn people Jeremiah has diligently tried to change. In frustration, the prophet asks whether these persons can ever be changed.

❑ *Jeremiah 15:13-14.* These verses seem to us to be out of place in the midst of the prophet's outcry. Perhaps these words belong with 17:3-4.

❑ *Jeremiah 15:18.* "A spring that fails" refers to springs that run freely through the rainy season but dry up in summer when the people really need them.

DIMENSION THREE:
WHAT DOES THE BIBLE MEAN TO ME?

In Chapters 12–15 we have seen Jeremiah facing some very tough questions. These difficult questions involve good and evil, blessing and suffering, reward and punishment. And they are doubly difficult because they all raise doubts about God's reliability. Such questions are not neatly answered in Scripture or anywhere else. They are the hard, lonely, nagging questions that each person must wrestle with in his or her own way. We hope the discussion aids below will help as you, too, take up this struggle.

Jeremiah 12:1-6
Why Does the Way of the Wicked Prosper?

An auto plant worker steals parts to build his son a racing car. The boy soon comes home with a substantial cash prize. A daughter, through lies, convinces her aged parents to disinherit her brother. In time she inherits their entire fortune. A doctor with a soothing manner prescribes frequent, expensive, and worthless treatments or surgery. His large income gives him a huge house and yearly vacations abroad. None of these wrongdoers suffers any obvious misfortune. How do cases like these make you feel?

We might expect that God, who is both righteous and just, should reward the good person and punish the evil person. Does God, in fact, do this? Does sin come back eventually to ensnare the evildoer?

Jeremiah 15:10-12, 15-18—Why Is My Pain Unending?

Read again Jeremiah 15:10-12, 15-18. Imagine yourself in the prophet's place. Then express his feelings in your own words.

Over the years people have developed many theories to explain why God allows the innocent to suffer. You have probably heard several of these theories, so list as many as you can. Then choose from among them those you find most helpful.

Jeremiah 14:7-11, 19-22; 15:1
The Problem of the Praying People

Have you ever known someone who made a mistake, repented, then continued to suffer the consequences of the earlier error? If so, share that person's experience with the class (omitting names, of course).

Now picture God as a loving parent. Can you think of any reason why God would not rescue these, his children, from their suffering?

Jeremiah 15:18
Will You Be to Me Like a Deceptive Brook?

Behind all the previous problems lurks that other nagging question: Can we really depend on God? Is this God consistent, reliable, trustworthy? If the answer is even a partial yes, then for what can we depend on God?

Food for Thought

You may well find yourself leaving this session with more questions than answers. And those questions may recur repeatedly during the days ahead. Ponder them. Reconsider your old answers. Try on some new answers for size. But do not let life come to a halt because you do not have a completely satisfactory solution. These are questions one can struggle and grow with for a lifetime.

O LORD, you deceived me,
and I was deceived (20:7).

5

God, You've Tricked Me
Jeremiah 16–20

DIMENSION ONE:
WHAT DOES THE BIBLE SAY?

Answer these questions by reading Jeremiah 16

1. What does God forbid Jeremiah to do, and why? (16:1-4)

2. God tells Jeremiah to stay away from two kinds of situations. What are they? (16:5, 8)

3. What point will Jeremiah make by his nonparticipation? (16:5, 9)

4. Why is God bringing evil upon the people? (16:10-12)

Answer these questions by reading Jeremiah 17

5. Where is Judah's sin written, and with what instruments is it engraved? (17:1)

6. What does Jeremiah ask God to do? (17:14, 17, 18)

Answer these questions by reading Jeremiah 18

7. What does Jeremiah see at the potter's house, and what does this signify to him? (18:3-9)

8. What plot have some persons laid, and why? (18:18)

9. What good thing has Jeremiah done for these plotters? (18:20)

10. What does Jeremiah now pray will happen to the plotters? (18:21-23)

Answer these questions by reading Jeremiah 19

11. What dramatic action does God ask Jeremiah to perform? (19:1-2, 10)

12. What does this jar smashing signify? (19:10-11)

Answer these questions by reading Jeremiah 20

13. Who is Pashhur, and what does he do when he hears Jeremiah's prophecies? (20:1-2)

14. How does Jeremiah respond to this treatment? (20:3-6)

15. In his anger, what does Jeremiah accuse God of? (20:7)

16. How are people responding to Jeremiah's prophecies? (20:7, 10)

17. What kind of message has God entrusted to Jeremiah? (20:8)

18. How has Jeremiah tried to relieve his misery, and what has been the result? (20:9)

19. What does Jeremiah count on to see him through? (20:11)

DIMENSION TWO:
WHAT DOES THE BIBLE MEAN?

The passages for this session include many diverse, discon-nected pieces. But from these passages we gain the following three inescapable impressions: (1) Jeremiah's entire life and being were taken up in obedience to God. (2) His prophecies brought Jeremiah frequent derision and persecution. (3) He suffered so much pain and frustration that he sometimes exploded in sheer anger.

❏ *Jeremiah 16.* This chapter begins with an explanation of some facts about Jeremiah's life. First, he never married. Second, he refused to comfort the bereaved or to participate in celebrations. The remainder of the chapter contains miscel-laneous small pieces whose origins are uncertain.

❏ *Jeremiah 16:1-13.* In this autobiographical passage we un-cover some unhappy dimensions of Jeremiah's life. He was forbidden to marry, to offer comfort to the bereaved, or to join in any feasting or celebrating. These problems, added to the unwelcome nature of his message, made his life a lonely one indeed. Yet Jeremiah obediently lived in this isolated fashion because he saw his personal life as part of his message. His actions had to illustrate his words. Since those words were words of impending doom, Jeremiah avoided doing anything that might indicate hope for the future.

Note that cutting oneself and shaving the head appear in verse 6 as common mourning customs. Deuteronomy 14:1 forbids such rituals. But the people were apparently practicing them anyway.

❏ *Jeremiah 17.* This chapter is another miscellaneous collec-tion of materials. Some of these passages are notes of later editors and writers. In those portions most certainly coming from the prophet himself (see verses 1-4, 9-10, 14-18), we see again his outspoken opposition to sin, his despair over the human heart, and his own personal suffering.

❏ *Jeremiah 17:1.* This verse offers another fine example of Jeremiah's imaginative use of metaphor. Here the prophet compares Judah's persistent sinfulness to words permanently engraved. These words are engraved with the hardest known instruments so they cannot be erased easily. Thus he pictures a sin deeply embedded both in individual hearts and institutional religion.

❏ *Jeremiah 17:2-3a.* Asherah poles were wooden representations of the goddess Asherah. This passage may indicate Jeremiah's continuing concern with idolatry. Or, the passage may be an editorial addition.

❏ *Jeremiah 17:13.* The names of those who forsake God will be written in the earth where they will soon be washed or blown away. The memory of these people will disappear, while the names of the faithful will remain in the Lord's book of life.

❏ *Jeremiah 17:14-18.* This prayer is one of Jeremiah's most poignant prayers. He is obviously suffering and tormented by those who mock his prophetic gifts or imply that he has lost them entirely. Apparently some persons are also accusing him of praying for the evil that he is, in fact, only announcing. Worst of all, Jeremiah fears that God, too, might turn against him. He pleads with God to be his refuge, not another tormentor. But, as usual, Jeremiah cannot envision satisfaction without revenge. So he also prays for the destruction of his enemies.

❏ *Jeremiah 17:19-27.* Most scholars consider this passage the work of an unknown writer. While Jeremiah probably supported the observance of sabbath laws, it is hard to imagine him making such a point of them as we find here. In fact, much of his preaching dwells upon the ways that merely keeping rules does not please God. But this author promises that keeping the sabbath will ensure Jerusalem's life forever.

❏ *Jeremiah 18.* In this chapter we learn of insights gained at a potter's house and of a plot against Jeremiah. The chapter also contains a poem decrying Israel's sin and another vindictive prayer against Jeremiah's enemies.

❏ *Jeremiah 18:1-12.* Jeremiah tells here of his visit to the potter's house. There he observed a craftsman at his daily work. The scene was a common enough one, but it held for Jeremiah some significant insights concerning Israel's relationship with God. Jeremiah suddenly saw Israel as something like the clay. It is material under God's, the Master Potter's, control. The Lord could make and break. God could shape the nation as

God willed. If the clay was unsuited for the original vessel, God could destroy that marred effort and fashion something else. Unlike some of Jeremiah's words, this message does not suggest the total destruction and abandonment of Israel.

❑ *Jeremiah 18:13-17.* This poem emphasizes the unnaturalness of Israel's sin. The "rocky slopes" (18:14—"crags of Sirion" in the NRSV) possibly refers to the peak of Mount Hermon, which is often covered with snow.

❑ *Jeremiah 18:18.* This verse tells us of a plot against Jeremiah. From this verse alone it is hard to tell what the plotters intended to do other than to slander and to discredit him. They may have hoped to arrange a capital charge against him, since verse 20 suggests an indirect effort to take the prophet's life. One ancient manuscript reads, "Let us listen to all his words." This reading indicates a plan, not of outright slander, but of listening until the prophet said something that could be twisted into a chargeable offense.

❑ *Jeremiah 18:19-23.* Again Jeremiah cries out for punishment of his enemies. We can see here and elsewhere how vicious Jeremiah could become in his anger.

❑ *Jeremiah 19.* This chapter tells of two messages, one an acted-out parable, the other a sermon. Unfortunately, they have been mixed together so that the sermon (19:2b-9) stands in the middle of the parable account (19:1-2a, 10-13).

❑ *Jeremiah 19:2.* The Potsherd Gate was apparently near the dump where potters threw their broken pieces of pottery. What an appropriate spot for the demonstration Jeremiah had in mind!

❑ *Jeremiah 20.* This chapter reveals in some detail the personal suffering Jeremiah endured because of his faithfulness to God. First we learn of a night spent in prison. Then we enter the more terrifying prison of the soul where Jeremiah must wrestle with his own anger and doubt.

❑ *Jeremiah 20:1-6.* The response to Jeremiah's words was not good. Pashhur, a priest charged with maintaining order in the Temple, seized Jeremiah, beat him (or had him beaten), and placed him in stocks overnight. Few in authority thought Jeremiah's words were really those of God. His ideas were disturbing, perhaps even sacrilegious; and he had to be punished for them. Note Jeremiah's reaction, however. A night in the stocks certainly did not intimidate him!

❑ *Jeremiah 20:7-9.* Something, though, could bring Jeremiah to the breaking point. These verses reveal what that something was. Here Jeremiah cries out in heart-rending anguish. He is torn with inner conflicts and doubts. He is terribly unsure of the very foundation upon which he has based his entire life. He is unsure of God. He has given up even the simplest joys of home and family, endured derision, stood up against the powerful religious establishment, even risked his life to serve a God he believed would bless and protect him. Yet all he has gained is a life of suffering. He becomes embittered. He determines not to speak God's word again. But to his chagrin he finds that he is so deeply committed that he cannot break away. He shouts his bitter accusations at God. But despite his anger, he finds he is bound by a relationship and a faith too deep to be destroyed. Even in anger and doubt he is still God's.

❑ *Jeremiah 20:10.* "Terror on every side!" was one of Jeremiah's favorite phrases. Some have suggested that it had even become an unkind nickname for him. ("Here comes old 'Terror on every side!' ")

❑ *Jeremiah 20:13.* This verse has a very different tone from those around it and is probably a separate piece placed here by an editor. The verse shows that, even in his anguish and doubt, Jeremiah never completely lost faith.

❑ *Jeremiah 20:14-18.* This poem, similar in thought to Jeremiah 15:10, reflects Jeremiah's awful despair. The towns (verse 16) are Sodom and Gomorrah.

DIMENSION THREE:
WHAT DOES THE BIBLE MEAN TO ME?

In this session we have plunged with Jeremiah into the darkest depths of his soul. We have suffered with the prophet through external persecution and inner despair. We have witnessed his angry accusations at the God whom he feared had deserted him. Do any of Jeremiah's experiences speak to our own situations? The questions below should help you explore that possibility.

Jeremiah 18:18-21; 20:1-10, 14-18
Suffering: The Reward of the Faithful?

Is suffering normal for God's faithful people, or was Jeremiah's experience rather unusual? Why?

Does it seem unfair to you that those who serve God most faithfully sometimes suffer the deepest hurts? How could this fact affect a person's ability to trust God?

Jeremiah 20:7-10—Being Angry With God

What situations can you imagine that might make you feel angry or resentful toward God?

What courses of action are open to someone who feels this kind of resentment?

In his anger, Jeremiah resolved to turn his back on God. Can you imagine yourself doing what Jeremiah did? How do you think you might feel if you did?

Jeremiah 20:1-7, 14-18
There's Pain, and Then There's Pain

Jeremiah encountered two different kinds of suffering. One was the public shame and physical brutality of his beating and imprisonment. The other was the inner suffering of anger, resentment, and doubt. Consider Jeremiah's response to each. Which do you think is easier to endure? Do you expect to face one or both kinds of suffering someday?

Food for Thought

Do resentments or outright anger sometimes creep into your relationship with God? If so, think a bit this week about those times. Then remember Jeremiah. Can you too trust enough to take that anger or resentment directly to that same God?

Hear the word of the LORD, O king of Judah,
you who sit on David's throne (22:2).

—— 6 ——

Listen, You Leaders

Jeremiah 21–25

DIMENSION ONE:
WHAT DOES THE BIBLE SAY?

Answer these questions by reading Jeremiah 21

1. Who has sent the two men to Jeremiah, and why? (21:1-2)

2. What does Jeremiah tell the men? (21:3-7)

Answer these questions by reading Jeremiah 22

3. What does God expect of a king? (22:3)

4. What will happen if Judah's king obeys God? (22:4-5)

5. For whom should the people weep? (22:10-12)

6. On whom does Jeremiah call forth woe? (22:13)

7. What is this man's foolish measure of greatness? (22:15)

8. What proper kingly qualities did this man's father have? (22:5-16)

9. What sort of man is this man instead? (22:17)

10. What is this king's name? (22:18)

11. What fate awaits this disobedient king? (22:18-19)

12. What does God intend to do to Jehoiachin (also known as Coniah) and his descendants? (22:24-27, 30)

5/21/05

Answer these questions by reading Jeremiah 23

13. With whom is the Lord angry and why? (23:1-2)

14. What kind of king will God raise up at some future day? (23:5-6)

15. How does the Lord's word concerning the prophets make Jeremiah feel? (23:9)

16. What have the prophets of Jerusalem done? (23:14)

17. What false words have these prophets spoken? (23:16-17)

18. What kinds of prophets does the Lord oppose? (23:30-32)

Answer this question by reading Jeremiah 24

19. What vision does Jeremiah see, and what does it mean? (24:1-5, 8)

Answer these questions by reading Jeremiah 25

20. Who must drink from the cup of the Lord's wrath? (25:15)

21. For whom have the days of slaughter and dispersion come? (25:34)

DIMENSION TWO: WHAT DOES THE BIBLE MEAN?

These chapters reflect Jeremiah's involvement in the political events of his time. Many of the passages we find here were spoken directly to the kings of Judah. Jeremiah had a special message for each one who reigned during his career. And again and again he repeated the Lord's essential demand of national leaders. God demands the kings reign in justice and righteousness, care for the poor and helpless, and never oppress the people whom they are supposed to protect.

President
Legislators
Governor
Councils+
Commissions

❑ *Jeremiah 21.* In this chapter we find Jeremiah's reply to an inquiry by King Zedekiah, a reminder of God's demands issued to an unnamed king, and a declaration of God's determination to punish his people.

❑ *Jeremiah 21:1-10.* This prose narrative tells of an incident that occurred during Nebuchadnezzar's siege of Jerusalem in 589 B.C.–587 B.C. King Zedekiah sent two deputies to ask Jeremiah if he had any word from God concerning this frightful situation. Jeremiah, in all honesty, could say no more than he had been saying all along: God intends to destroy Jerusalem. (See especially verse 10.)

Pashhur, one of the deputies, is not the same Pashhur who beat and imprisoned Jeremiah (Chapter 20). They are from different families, and this one may or may not be a priest.

"Nebuchadrezzar" in the NRSV (verse 2) is an alternate spelling for Nebuchadnezzar.

❑ *Jeremiah 21:11-12.* Jeremiah delivered God's word to the kings of Judah whether or not he was asked to do so. This brief speech, which was probably unsolicited, summarizes what God expects of a ruler. It also makes clear God's intention to enforce his demands.

LISTEN, YOU LEADERS   **47**

The phrase "every morning" would not mean that court should be held only in the A.M. (although that practice may have been customary). The phrase simply means justice should be done promptly or daily.

❏ *Jeremiah 21:13-14.* This poem directed toward an unnamed city is another example of Jeremiah's warning of destruction to come.

❏ *Jeremiah 22.* This chapter continues the collection of messages to kings.

❏ *Jeremiah 22:1-9.* Here again Jeremiah outlines the obligations of a Davidic king. The kings of Judah are not to be powerful, privileged tyrants. They are God's agents. They are to establish and oversee a society where justice and righteousness prevail for all.

❏ *Jeremiah 22:10-12.* This lament mourns the exile of Shallum (Jehoahaz). This king reigned only a few months after his father, Josiah, was killed by the Egyptians at the battle of Megiddo. Pharaoh Neco soon replaced Jehoahaz with his brother, Jehoiakim, who was apparently more receptive to Egyptian control.

❏ *Jeremiah 22:13-19.* Here Jeremiah denounced King Jehoiakim in no uncertain terms. Jehoiakim does not meet Jeremiah's criteria for a good king. He had built a great palace using slave labor. His extravagance has strained the nation's economy. He is greedy, dishonest, oppressive, and violent—scarcely God's just and righteous ideal!

Verse 15, in particular, strikes at the heart of Jeremiah's concern. What is the mark of real leadership? Is it wealth and show, or is it the effective guidance of a just society? Jeremiah obviously believes that Jehoiakim has adopted the shallower, materialistic definition of kingship and that this outlook will spell his own and his nation's doom.

Notice that the common citizen in verse 13 is the king's neighbor. The people are not an expendable labor force provided for the king's convenience. They are human beings, his neighbors over whose time and effort he has no special claim. The king has, instead, the obligation to respect each person and to treat everyone as one should treat a neighbor.

❑ *Jeremiah 22:20-23.* This poem again warns the people of disaster to come.

Lebanon, Bashan, and Abarim are three high-altitude areas. (Lebanon and Abarim are mountainous regions. Bashan is a plateau.) Lebanon was noted for its cedar trees. Many of these trees were used in constructing the Jerusalem temple and palace. So those who lived in the royal complex were indeed "nestled in cedar buildings."

❑ *Jeremiah 22:24-30.* Here Jeremiah announces the doom of yet another king. This one is Jehoiachin (Coniah), who reigned only three months before surrendering to Nebuchadnezzar (598 B.C.). Jehoiachin and many leading citizens were deported to Babylon. Zedekiah succeeded him on the throne in Judah.

The term *childless* in verse 30 should not suggest that Jehoiachin had no children. He actually had seven sons. But, as a king, he may as well have had none; for none ever succeeded to the throne. (Zerubbabel, Jehoiachin's grandson, did rule for a time as governor, not king, under Persian auspices.)

❑ *Jeremiah 23.* In this chapter we find Jeremiah addressing groups of political and religious leaders instead of specific kings. The speeches come from various times in Jeremiah's career. But the same note of responsibility for the people's welfare runs throughout the speeches.

❑ *Jeremiah 23:1-2.* The word *shepherds* could refer to kings or to any national leaders. With this image Jeremiah again emphasizes the leader's role in caring for the people. The leaders here have apparently promoted disorder by their foolish policies. They have exposed the people to danger rather than bringing them together and protecting them as God intended.

❑ *Jeremiah 23:5-6.* "The LORD Our Righteousness" involves a play on the name *Zedekiah,* which means Yahweh is my righteousness. The term *righteousness* may also mean salvation or vindication. So the message of this passage is that at some future time God will raise up a king who will save his people and fulfill the promise of Zedekiah's name.

❑ *Jeremiah 23:7-8.* These verses duplicate Jeremiah 16:14-15. They probably have been added by a later writer offering hope to the exiles in Babylon.

❏ *Jeremiah 23:9-40.* In these oracles Jeremiah turns to the religious leaders, the prophets and priests. They, too, are responsible for leading the people rightly. And they, too, have turned aside from their responsibilities for an easier path. What is worse, they have taken lightly their special relationship with God and have spoken their own thoughts in his name. For this they must be condemned.

In verse 33 Jeremiah uses one of his many word plays to emphasize his message. This time the word (as it appears in the NRSV) is "burden." The NIV translates this same word as "oracle." A prophetic word was sometimes referred to as "the burden of the Lord." It was a package, so to speak, that the prophet was compelled to carry from God to his people. But Jeremiah turns this pious phrase into a sharp condemnation. The people and their prophets are the burden. They are the heavy load that God is very tired of carrying.

❏ *Jeremiah 24.* This chapter concerns a vision that came during the reign of Zedekiah. One group of citizens had already been exiled to Babylon after the defeat in 597 B.C. Some of those left in Jerusalem apparently supposed they were favored by God. But Jeremiah insisted that they who remained were in fact more corrupt than those who were exiled.

❏ *Jeremiah 25.* This collection of oracles emphasizes God's coming punishment for the sins of Judah and other nations. This section concludes with a poem that again denounces decadent leaders and proclaims an awful fate for those who have betrayed their trust. Much of this material is probably a later expansion upon Jeremiah's words. However, the poem could well be original to Jeremiah.

❏ *Jeremiah 25:17-26.* This passage suggests that all nations and their leaders are under God's judgment. They must all bear his wrath.

Uz is an area somewhere to the east of Judah.

Tyre and Sidon are cities in Phoenicia.

Dedan and Tema are tribes inhabiting northwestern Arabia.

The exact locations of Buz and Zimri are unknown.

DIMENSION THREE:
WHAT DOES THE BIBLE MEAN TO ME?

In this session we have examined Jeremiah's understanding of responsible leadership. What implications do his words have for life in turn-of-the-millennium America? Use the questions below to help you think through some modern issues in light of Jeremiah's understanding.

Jeremiah 25:15-38—God Is Over All the Nations

Do you believe, as Jeremiah did, that all nations and their leaders are directly responsible to God for the kinds of societies they develop? Do you think most national leaders believe this? Do representatives of the news media seem to believe it? Does the average voter? What recent public comments can you recall that referred to a leader's responsibility toward God?

Jeremiah 22:1-5, 13-17; 23:1-6
How Can We Fulfill God's Commands?

Reread Jeremiah 22:1-5, 13-17; 23:1-6. In modern terms, what are the really essential qualities God expects of a leader? What qualities and practices does God abhor? Can you think of any current situations where leaders are acting as God intends?

Could failing to follow God's guidelines cause a leader or a nation to fall? If so, how?

We live in a nation of extreme religious diversity. Sometimes during election campaigns a candidate who is known to be an active member of a religious group will be questioned on the role his or her religion will play in public policy. Often, trying to appear fair and open, such a candidate will proclaim that his or her religion will have no influence at all. How do you feel about such a statement? Would you feel the same whether the candidate's faith was similar to or quite different from your own?

When conflict arises, should a public official act according to conscience or according to the will of the majority

We live in a democratic nation, one in which ultimate responsibility lies with the citizens themselves. We also live in a nation that espouses the principle of separation of church and state. As God's people we know that he wants the nation (and the world) to operate according to his intent. Other citizens, however, do not share this view. Should Christians, then, campaign for programs that reflect what they believe are God's wishes? If so, what methods should Christians use to influence national policy? (Compare, for example, voting, lobbying, advertising campaigns, civil disobedience, and force.)

Should all citizens be taught the Bible in school so that they would know what God expects and could vote or lead from that knowledge? How about the *Koran* and the *Book of Mormon*? Should school children study those books, too?

Food for Thought

Jeremiah was clear enough about what God expects of national leaders. But what can we do, as citizens in a diverse, democratic society, to encourage the kind of leadership God intends for us? That is a big question—one that has caused much controversy, both within the church and in the public at large. Notice how often this issue comes up in the week ahead, and try to formulate some answers of your own to the problems involved.

Do not listen to the words of the prophets . . .
they are prophesying lies (27:14).

7

Listen to the Real Word of God

Jeremiah 26–30

DIMENSION ONE:
WHAT DOES THE BIBLE SAY?

Answer these questions by reading Jeremiah 26

1. When do the main events in this chapter take place? (26:1)

2. What does God tell Jeremiah to do? (26:2)

3. What do the people who hear Jeremiah do? (26:8-9)

4. How does Jeremiah answer the charges against him? (26:12-15)

5. What judgment do the officials hand down? (26:16)

6. What additional explanation do the elders offer for this decision? (26:17-19)

7. What had happened to Uriah in a similar situation? (26:21-23)

Answer these questions by reading Jeremiah 27

8. Under what king do the events in this chapter occur? (27:1)

9. What object does God tell Jeremiah to make? (27:2)

10. What does Jeremiah say to the envoys, to Zedekiah, and to the priests and people? (27:6-9, 12, 16-17)

11. What challenge does Jeremiah offer the optimistic prophets? (27:18)

Answer these questions by reading Jeremiah 28

12. What prophetic message does Hananiah bring? (28:2)

13. What argument does Jeremiah raise against the validity of Hananiah's message? (28:8)

14. When will the people know that a prophecy of peace is valid? (28:9)

15. What symbolic action does Hananiah perform, and what does he mean to show by it? (28:10-11)

16. When and how does Jeremiah respond to Hananiah's action? (28:12-13, 15-16)

Answer these questions by reading Jeremiah 29

17. To whom has Jeremiah written a letter? (29:1)

18. What advice does Jeremiah give? (29:5-9)

19. What will God do to the prophets Ahab and Zedekiah, and why? (29:21-23)

20. What complaint has Shemaiah lodged with Zephaniah? (29:24-28)

21. What does Zephaniah do when he receives Shemaiah's letter? (29:29)

22. What word does Jeremiah send the exiles concerning Shemaiah? (29:31-32)

Answer these questions by reading Jeremiah 30

23. What hope does God offer the people? (30:3, 18)

24. To what natural phenomenon does Jeremiah compare God's wrath? (30:23)

DIMENSION TWO:
WHAT DOES THE BIBLE MEAN?

Most of this session's material tells of specific incidents in Jeremiah's life. Each incident involves a conflict with religious leaders. And each reveals the prophet's tenacity and courage in defending the true prophetic word. With Chapter 30, however, we move beyond these incidents and begin a mixed collection known as the "Book of Consolation."

❑ *Jeremiah 26.* Chapter 26 reports a nearly fatal incident that occurred quite early in Jeremiah's career.

❑ *Jeremiah 26:2.* One wonders if Jeremiah might have felt tempted to omit a harsh word or two.

❑ *Jeremiah 26:4-6.* This is the basic message Jeremiah was to deliver at the Temple. A longer version appears in Jeremiah 7:1-15. Unfortunately, we cannot be sure whether Jeremiah

7:1-15 is a later expansion or whether these verses are a summary of the original speech.

❏ *Jeremiah 26:9-10.* A lynching appears imminent. But someone, apparently caring that things be done legally, has called in the proper officials.

❏ *Jeremiah 26:20-23.* This story is not part of the preceding discussion but has been added by the editor to show that not all prophets were so fortunate as Micah and Jeremiah. Beyond this mention here we know nothing more of Uriah.

❏ *Jeremiah 27.* Several years have now passed. A new king sits on the throne of Judah. But Jeremiah continues to speak of God's punishment. He addresses a group of foreign ambassadors, King Zedekiah himself, and the priests and people generally. Each time, he insists that the Babylonian enemy is God's agent. And each time, Jeremiah warns against false prophecies that promise peace and victory.

❏ *Jeremiah 27:3.* Nebuchadnezzar had already conquered all of Palestine. But great unrest was evident throughout his empire. In Jerusalem, ambassadors from several small states had gathered to plan a rebellion. Jeremiah, with his striking visual aid, warns the envoys against this revolt. He insists that they should instead accept the yoke of subservience to Babylon and should resist any contrary counsels.

❏ *Jeremiah 27:19.* The "Sea" is a basin that was used in the Temple. The Sea, the pillars, and the stands were among the more valuable Temple furnishings.

❏ *Jeremiah 27:20.* Jehoiachin was the king who surrendered to Nebuchadnezzar just three months after his father's death in 598 B.C.

❏ *Jeremiah 28.* At about this same time Jeremiah came into direct conflict with one particular opposing prophet. Chapter 28 offers us a detailed account of this conflict.

❏ *Jeremiah 28:6-9.* Jeremiah honestly wishes that Hananiah's cheerful prophecies would come true, but he knows they will not. He says so politely, then goes on to offer some criteria for judging contemporary prophecies. Contemporary prophecies should resemble valid prophecies from the past, or they must be proved correct by the passage of time.

❑ *Jeremiah 28:12-14.* Jeremiah takes some time to consider his response to Hananiah. Finally he realizes that he can use this humiliating event to state even more strongly God's determination to keep Judah under the Babylonian yoke.

❑ *Jeremiah 28:15-17.* Death was the prescribed penalty for a prophet uttering false prophecy. Here God himself is judge and executioner.

❑ *Jeremiah 29.* Jeremiah also attempted to advise those who had been carried off to Babylon. Here we find some of his correspondence with them. We also see the angry response of one exile who did not care for Jeremiah's advice.

❑ *Jeremiah 29:4-7.* Jeremiah advises the exiles to make themselves comfortable, for their stay in Babylon will be long. He even tells them to pray for their enemies and gives a very practical reason for doing so. He tells them that the prosperity of Babylon is to the exiles' advantage. Hardship for Babylon could only mean greater hardship for the captives.

This letter, along with other descriptions we have of exilic life, suggests that the captured people were not imprisoned or badly treated. They could buy land, build homes, and even start businesses. Their pain was not that of torture or physical deprivation, it was emotional and spiritual pain. They had lost their homes, their properties, their friends, and their families who remained behind in Judah. But worst of all, they had been carried from God's land. They were far from the Temple and, they feared, far from God's presence and power. Thus Jeremiah's call to pray for Babylon was doubly surprising. Some of the people probably were not even sure that God would hear them from so far away!

❑ *Jeremiah 29:8.* Again Jeremiah warns against false prophets.

❑ *Jeremiah 29:21-23.* Ahab and Zedekiah are two self-styled prophets among the exiles. Their obviously sinful behavior belies their claims to godly gifts.

This Zedekiah, whose father was Maaseiah, should not be confused with King Zedekiah. King Zedekiah's father was Josiah.

❑ *Jeremiah 29:24-29.* Shemaiah is apparently a leader within the community in Babylon. His letter to Zephaniah (Jeremiah 29:26-28) shows how very angry he is at Jeremiah's prophecies.

Zephaniah, the priest, is the same one who was sent to obtain Jeremiah's advice in Chapter 21. He seems to be a brother of the prophet Zedekiah whom Jeremiah so strongly condemns. Zephaniah, however, has not been exiled. He has remained in Jerusalem and has taken over Pashhur's old job as keeper of order in the Temple. Interestingly enough, the priest seems sympathetic to Jeremiah and does not punish him, even after Shemaiah's strong rebuke.

❏ *Jeremiah 29:30-32.* In another letter to the exiles, Jeremiah condemns Shemaiah. He, too, has spoken falsely in God's name.

❏ *Jeremiah 30.* This chapter contains numerous words of hope. Some of these words are from Jeremiah, and some are from other persons. The chapter marks the beginning of the "Book of Consolation."

❏ *Jeremiah 30:12-15, 23-24.* These passages include messages, not of hope, but of wrath. In some places additional notes have been added to the prophecies. These additional notations make the message of these verses more meaningful to those living after the fall of Jerusalem.

The storm image appears also in Jeremiah 23:19-20. This image makes an excellent vehicle for Jeremiah's thought. A storm conveys the idea of a powerful destructive force that cannot be stopped or controlled. One can only wait until the storm has passed.

DIMENSION THREE:
WHAT DOES THE BIBLE MEAN TO ME?

Jeremiah 26:8-9; 27:12-15; 28:10-15
When Prophets Disagree

On what political, social, or personal moral issues do religious leaders strongly disagree today?

These leaders all ostensibly serve the same God. How then do you explain their widely differing interpretations of God's will?

Jeremiah 29:21-23; 28:7-9
How Can You Tell Without a Scorecard?

Jeremiah makes a special point of Ahab and Zedekiah's adulteries. Jeremiah's words suggest that a would-be prophet's morality might help us judge the validity of his or her religious guidance. What do you think? Does immoral behavior prove that a religious leader's advice is not of God? Does an upright life prove that a leader's words come from God?

How else might you determine who is and who is not speaking God's word?

Jeremiah 28:12-16—What to Do?

Let's assume that you have determined what you believe to be God's will on a particular issue. Then you meet another Christian who flatly contradicts your assessment. What would you do or say? Would it make any difference if other people were overhearing the exchange?

Food for Thought

How can you tell who has the real word of God? How can you deal with those whom you are sure do not? These are difficult but vitally important questions. Notice this week how many conflicting pieces of religious guidance you hear. Notice, too, the criteria you yourself use for accepting or rejecting this advice. Then take a close look at how you deal with those whom you believe to be wrong.

I have loved you with an everlasting love;
I have drawn you with loving-kindness (31:3).

—— 8 ——
God's Love Still Holds
Jeremiah 31–35

DIMENSION ONE:
WHAT DOES THE BIBLE SAY?

Answer these questions by reading Jeremiah 31

1. Why has God continued his faithfulness to Israel? (31:1-3)

2. What good things does God promise for Israel? (31:4-5)

3. Whose voice is weeping, and why? (31:15)

4. With what promise does God comfort Rachel? (31:16-17)

5. What advice does Jeremiah offer the exiles? (31:21)

6. What new action is God planning? (31:31)

7. How will the new situation differ from the old? (31:33-34)

Answer these questions by reading Jeremiah 32

8. What crisis is occurring? (32:2)

9. Where is Jeremiah? (32:2-3)

10. What business transaction does Jeremiah carry out, and why? (32:9, 15)

Answer these questions by reading Jeremiah 33

11. What have the people had to do in order to defend the city? (33:4)

12. What are the Babylonians (also known as Chaldeans) going to do, and why? (33:5)

13. Into what condition does Jerusalem eventually fall? (33:10)

14. What does God promise? (33:6-9, 11)

Answer these questions by reading Jeremiah 34

15. What is Jeremiah's message to Zedekiah? (34:2-5)

16. What covenant have Zedekiah and the Israelites made, and with what result? (34:8-11)

17. What is Jeremiah's response to this turn of events? (34:17)

Answer these questions by reading Jeremiah 35

18. When do the events in this chapter take place? (35:1)

19. What does Jeremiah do with the Recabites, and how do they respond? (35:2-6)

20. Why are the Recabites in Jerusalem, and why is their presence there unusual? (35:7-11)

21. What lesson does Jeremiah draw from the Recabites' behavior? (35:16-18)

DIMENSION TWO:
WHAT DOES THE BIBLE MEAN?

Jeremiah, prophet of doom and destruction! Yes, he was definitely that. In this session we encounter still more warnings of the devastation that sin would bring. But doom and destruction, sin and punishment, were not the sum total of his message. Jeremiah was also a prophet of hope. This was no shallow "Maybe God will let us off the hook," however. His was a deep and unshakable hope based upon God's everlasting love and his power to forgive and to renew. In Jeremiah 31–35 we learn more about that hope.

❑ *Jeremiah 31.* This chapter ends the "Book of Consolation." The passages come from different periods, but they all reflect Jeremiah's faith that God would restore his people.

❑ *Jeremiah 31:2-6.* The word *Samaria* refers to the northern capital and its surrounding territory. Ephraim was a major tribe whose name eventually came to stand for all of the Northern Kingdom. This kingdom suffered Assyrian exile in 733 B.C. and final defeat in 721 B.C.

These geographical references may indicate that this and other oracles in Chapter 31 were first addressed to the northern tribes. If so, the oracles could date from as early as the time of Josiah.

❑ *Jeremiah 31:14.* "Satisfy the priests with abundance" suggests much worship activity and many sacrifices.

❑ *Jeremiah 31:15.* Jeremiah here pictures Rachel, mother of the northern tribes, haunting her grave in Ramah and weeping bitterly for her lost children.

❑ *Jeremiah 31:19.* "Beat my breast" (NIV) or "struck my thigh" (NRSV) is an expression of extreme grief.

❑ *Jeremiah 31:31-34.* This vision of a new covenant is one of Jeremiah's greatest contributions to our understanding of God. He acknowledges that the old covenant has been broken by Israel's persistent sin. The people have proved again and again that they are incapable of maintaining or even remembering their promises to God. God has punished them, hoping to bring them to repentance. Yet God still loves them and will not abandon them. He will make a new covenant, and he will alter the very hearts of his people so that they will keep it forever.

This new covenant hope has extended far beyond the sixth-century situation to which it first applied. For us it provides a basic framework for understanding the life, death, and resurrection of Jesus. This new covenant is so much a part of that understanding, in fact, that we call the collected writings concerning Jesus and his church the "New Testament" or "New Covenant."

❑ *Jeremiah 32.* This chapter reveals a striking and significant incident that took place immediately before the fall of Jerusalem. Jeremiah bought a field. He offered the purchase as an expression of his faith that God would one day restore the land and its people.

❑ *Jeremiah 32:2-5.* We learn in Jeremiah 37–38 a bit more about Jeremiah's imprisonment. The reason that was given for the imprisonment was Jeremiah's attempt to leave the city for a visit to Anathoth. A sentry assumed he was deserting and jailed him. But the editor is no doubt right in reporting Jeremiah's prophecies as the real, or underlying, reason for his detention.

❑ *Jeremiah 32:7.* The law provided that when a man was in danger of losing his land through poverty or debt, his next of kin had both the right and the responsibility to buy it. This would keep both the land and the financial aid within the family. This kind of law would also discourage real estate speculation and usury.

❑ *Jeremiah 33.* Here the editor has collected numerous additional prophecies that offered hope to a people faced with imminent or actual defeat.

❑ *Jeremiah 33:4.* This verse gives us an interesting glimpse of conditions within Jerusalem just before the city's fall. The people have had to tear down houses, even royal residences, either to obtain material to repair the wall or to build new defenses.

❑ *Jeremiah 33:5-9.* Here two apparently separate prophecies have been continued. Together they reveal a God who will do whatever is necessary for the good of his people. He will punish, and he will heal the children whom he loves.

❏ *Jeremiah 34.* With this chapter we shift back to an earlier point in the Babylonian campaign against Judah. Jeremiah is not yet in prison but is free to approach the king. As at other times, the prophet minces no words but bluntly tells Zedekiah what God intends and why.

❏ *Jeremiah 34:1-5.* Here Jeremiah repeats his basic interpretation of the Babylonian attack: It is God's doing. As for the king, he cannot escape Nebuchadnezzar but must face him as a rebel who dared try to break away from the empire's grasp. The underlying implication of this warning is that Zedekiah should resign himself to defeat. Trying to evade the plans of God is futile.

❏ *Jeremiah 34:8-22.* The timing of this word to Zedekiah is a bit more specific. When the Babylonians began the actual siege of Jerusalem, people became more frightened and less confident that God would automatically save the city. Grasping at straws, they decided to try to placate God by obeying a long-neglected law regarding slavery. Soon, however, the Egyptian army approached. The Babylonians could not maintain the Jerusalem siege and fight the Egyptians at the same time, so the siege was abandoned. The city's inhabitants, sure they had been miraculously saved, promptly took back their slaves. Naturally, Jeremiah was incensed and said so while warning that the battle with Babylon was far from over.

❏ *Jeremiah 35.* With this incident we again move backward, this time to the reign of Jehoiakim (609 B.C.–598 B.C.). Then, as later, Jeremiah felt great concern over the people's covenant faithlessness. This narrative shows the prophet using yet another unique public demonstration to get across his point that faithful obedience is both possible and essential.

❏ *Jeremiah 35:2.* The Recabites were founded by Jonadab, son of Recab, in the time of Jehu (842 B.C.–815 B.C.). Repelled by deep social and moral decay, these people determined to withdraw to the supposed purity of Israel's early desert life. They scorned houses in favor of tents, refused to plant crops, and drank no wine. (Wine was not used by the earlier Hebrews, probably because grapes were unavailable in the desert.)

DIMENSION THREE:
WHAT DOES THE BIBLE MEAN TO ME?

Israel had sinned. The sacred covenant was broken, with devastating consequences. Yet Jeremiah saw real hope for his despairing people. This hope was founded in the everlasting love of God. Could the insight and faith of this ancient prophet speak to any of us today? You can use the questions below to explore this possibility.

Jeremiah 34:13-18; 31:31-34
Covenants, Broken and Renewed

A covenant is an agreement, a kind of contract. Some religious covenants you may have entered into are confirmation, marriage, and baptism. What did you promise in each case? Who would suffer if the covenant were broken? In what ways would those persons suffer?

Can a broken contract, say a job contract, a building contract, or a marriage vow, be renegotiable? How? By whom? Would there be a cost involved? Would the new relationship be exactly like the old one? If not, how would it be different?

We have one Christian ceremony designed especially to deal with the broken relationship between God and his covenant people. What is the ceremony, and how does it heal the breach between God and persons?

Jeremiah 33:10-11
What Does a Broken Covenant Feel Like?

Here are two examples of broken covenants:

1. Don, a confirmed church member, has just been fired for poor job performance due to alcoholism. The bank is about to repossess his car for missed payments. He has not been to church or offered private prayer for over ten years.

2. Marcia has been discovered in an extramarital affair. Her husband has moved out. Her lover has left town.

GOD'S LOVE STILL HOLDS **67**

Both Don and Marcia see the folly of their behavior. What covenants were broken in each case? What circumstances or feelings in these examples might correspond to Jeremiah 33:10?

Jeremiah 31:2-5, 15-17, 31-37—Is There Any Hope?

Consider the following situation: John and Rosemary entered into a covenant with God when they presented their two-month-old daughter, Karen, for baptism. They did not immediately begin attending worship, feeling that the baby was too small to understand or would cry in church. One year followed another. They meant to teach Karen a table grace and later to explain some of the church's moral expectations, but they never got around to it. In almost no time Karen was in college, experimenting with drugs, and pregnant.

Let's assume that John and Rosemary are old friends of yours now living in another city. They have written to you of their guilt and despair over Karen. Using Jeremiah 31:2-5, 15-17, 31-37, write a letter of hope and faith to them.

How might John and Rosemary feel if they finally came to believe in the everlasting love Jeremiah speaks of?

In the midst of a war Jeremiah purchased a field. What action(s) would similarly express faith in God's forgiving and renewing love to Don, Marcia, John, Rosemary, or Karen?

Food for Thought

This week you will probably encounter, personally or through the news, several tragic human stories. Ask yourself what Jeremiah's words might mean to the persons involved.

*So Jeremiah took another scroll and gave it to the scribe
Baruch . . . [who] wrote on it all the words of
the scroll that Jehoiakim . . . burned in the fire (36:32).*

9

With Jaws Firmly Set
Jeremiah 36–40

DIMENSION ONE:
WHAT DOES THE BIBLE SAY?

Answer these questions by reading Jeremiah 36

1. What does God tell Jeremiah to do? (36:2)

2. What does God hope to accomplish? (36:3)

3. What does Baruch do for Jeremiah? (36:4-6, 8)

4. What do the officials decide to do about the reading, and
   what advice do they give Baruch? (36:16-19)

5. What does Jehoiakim do with the scroll, and what command does he give? (36:23, 26)

6. What does Jeremiah do next? (36:32)

Answer these questions by reading Jeremiah 37

7. What god-fearing king is given to the Israelites by Nebuchadnezzar? (37:1-3)

8. What military action has just taken place? (37:5)

9. What does Jeremiah tell Zedekiah concerning this situation? (37:6-10)

10. What does Jeremiah try to do, and what happens? (37:11-15)

11. What is the charge against him? (37:13)

12. What further word does Jeremiah give Zedekiah, and what request does the prophet make? (37:17-20)

13. How does Zedekiah respond? (37:21)

Answer these questions by reading Jeremiah 38

14. What additional charge do the officials bring against Jeremiah? (38:4)

15. What is Zedekiah's reply? (38:5)

16. What do the officials do to Jeremiah, and how is he rescued? (38:6-13)

17. What does Jeremiah tell Zedekiah to do? (38:17-18)

18. What excuse does Zedekiah ask Jeremiah to give for their conversation? (38:26)

Answer these questions by reading Jeremiah 39

19. How does the siege of Jerusalem end? (39:1-3, 8-10)

20. What becomes of Zedekiah? (39:4-7)

21. What do the Babylonians do with Jeremiah? (39:11-14)

Answer these questions by reading Jeremiah 40

22. In this account where does Nebuzaradan find Jeremiah? (40:1)

23. What choice does Nebuzaradan offer, and which option does Jeremiah choose? (40:4-6)

24. Who is the new governor of Judah, and what rumor does he hear? (40:7, 13-14)

DIMENSION TWO:
WHAT DOES THE BIBLE MEAN?

Life can be difficult for the person who insists upon speaking an uncomfortable, unwelcome truth. And, if society turns unstable through dissension or war, "difficult" can become just plain "dangerous." The incidents we find in Jeremiah 36–40 show all too clearly the dangers Jeremiah faced in faithfully continuing to speak God's word. But they show, too, the magnificent determination and courage of this steely prophet.

❑ *Jeremiah 36.* This incident from early in Jeremiah's career shows both the serious conflict his prophecies generated and his persistence in the face of those conflicts.

❑ *Jeremiah 36:1.* The date is 606 B.C.–605 B.C.

❑ *Jeremiah 36:4.* Baruch served as Jeremiah's secretary, companion, and friend. He appeared previously in Jeremiah 32:12-13, 16, where we see him assisting in the legalities of the land purchase. Many scholars suspect that Baruch not only wrote down Jeremiah's prophecies but also recorded much of the biographical information we find in the Book of Jeremiah.

❑ *Jeremiah 36:11-12.* Gemariah is apparently a brother of the Ahikam who had earlier helped save the prophet from a mob (Jeremiah 26:24). Micaiah is Gemariah's son. Again and again we shall see these and other members of the family of Shaphan helping Jeremiah.

Note that Elnathan is the same Elnathan who brought Uriah back from Egypt for trial and execution (Jeremiah 26:20-23). Elnathan has either changed his mind about prophets like Jeremiah and Uriah, or he was simply following orders in the earlier incident. Perhaps he did not fully realize what the outcome might be.

Of the remaining men, nothing further is known.

❑ *Jeremiah 36:16-25.* These officials do not wish Jeremiah any trouble. In fact, they do all they can to help by trying to safeguard the scroll and by warning Baruch to hide. But they decide that the king must be told. Perhaps they hope he will heed the Lord's word. Or perhaps they fear that Jehoiakim will learn of the reading anyway and will question why his officials did not report it. The results are disastrous but probably unavoidable.

❑ *Jeremiah 37–40.* These chapters tell us in some detail what happened to Jeremiah during the awful days just before and just after the fall of Jerusalem.

❑ *Jeremiah 37:1.* Zedekiah (597 B.C.–587 B.C.) is now king. The events reported here, however, all occur toward the end of his reign, in 588 B.C. and 587 B.C.

❑ *Jeremiah 37:12.* The words *to get his share* are unclear in the Hebrew and have been translated in a variety of ways. We cannot be sure just what Jeremiah intended to do. It would appear, though, that he had planned to take care of some family business in Anathoth.

❑ *Jeremiah 37:16-21.* This secret interview shows Zedekiah for the weak leader that he was. He valued Jeremiah's prophecies. But he was so afraid of opposition, he had to consult the prophet secretly. The ration of bread indicates a real personal concern. Yet Zedekiah could not go so far as to release the prophet, nor would the king ever actually follow Jeremiah's advice.

❑ *Jeremiah 38:1-3.* Gedaliah may be the son of the Pashhur who had earlier had Jeremiah beaten. (See Jeremiah 20:1-6.) Jehucal is the Jehucal of Jeremiah 37:3. Pashhur, who was the son of Malkijah, appears as one of the deputies sent to Jeremiah in 21:1.

❑ *Jeremiah 38:5.* Nowhere is Zedekiah's weakness more obvious. He admits he has no power to stop the princes and makes no effort to do so.

❑ *Jeremiah 39:14.* This Gedaliah's father was Ahikam, the man who saved Jeremiah from the mob (Jeremiah 26:24). His uncle Gemariah was one of the princes who urged Jehoiakim not to burn the scroll (Jeremiah 36:25)

❑ *Jeremiah 39:15-18.* This section is apparently out of place chronologically. (Jeremiah is still in prison here.) It probably should follow the cistern incident. Some scholars believe this passage is a later addition.

❑ *Jeremiah 40:1-6.* Here we find a second account of how Jeremiah fared when the city fell. Although the two versions differ on some details, they agree that the Babylonians did show some concern for Jeremiah and that he eventually came under Gedaliah's care.

❑ *Jeremiah 40:7-10.* Gedaliah, appointed governor by the Babylonians, tries to restore peace, order, and a measure of civic harmony. Apparently some of Israel's soldiers outside Jerusalem have avoided capture and are making isolated raids here and there. The towns they have recaptured are probably deserted ones, abandoned by the victorious Babylonians.

Mizpah, the provisional capital, is about eight miles north of the destroyed Jerusalem.

DIMENSION THREE:
WHAT DOES THE BIBLE MEAN TO ME?

As the war ground to its grim but inevitable close, Jeremiah's personal situation grew more and more perilous. Yet the events in these chapters show us a prophet who had the courage, the endurance, and the persistence to continue speaking God's word despite the frustrations and the very real dangers involved.

For many of us, ancient battles, imprisonments in besieged cities, and life-and-death decisions of international import may seem far away, even unreal. But are the issues behind these events really so remote? Use the questions below to explore some ways these issues might touch you more personally.

Jeremiah 36:25-26; 37:11-15; 38:4, 13, 19
Wanted: People of Courage

Arrests, beatings, dungeons, cisterns—they all sound pretty frightful, not at all the sort of thing one looks forward to in the process of obeying God. Yet people are inconvenienced, harassed, tortured, and killed for doing what they believe God wants them to. What contemporary examples can you cite? Can you think of any issues that, if pursued, could lead you into difficult waters? Share those issues with the group.

Some people demonstrate a great deal of courage under pressure; others do not. This session's readings show not only Jeremiah but also Elnathan, Delaiah, Gemariah, Ebed-Melech, and others as persons of courage. Zedekiah, by contrast, appears to be especially weak. What makes the difference? What factors lead one person to stand firm while another waffles and wavers?

Zedekiah is a person of particular interest because he is ostensibly the most powerful Judean in many of this session's events. But he seems the least able to carry through his convictions. What do you think? Is it easier or harder for persons in positions of power to act courageously on their beliefs?

Jeremiah 36:27-32; 38:14-23
Persistence, a Special Form of Courage

When have you seen someone join a church or charitable group, volunteer to do all kinds of work, then disappear after a few weeks? Jeremiah was obviously far from this type of hot-and-cold do-gooder. But his kind of persistence is not easy to imitate. What might discourage a person from sticking with a worthy cause over the long haul?

Which is more difficult, to show courage in a painful but short-lived situation or through a long series of frustrations?

Jeremiah 38:1-4, 17-20
Some Call It Courage; Others Call It Treason

Many people saw Jeremiah's words as treasonous. Do you suppose his preaching did weaken his nation in time of war? Do you believe he was disloyal to his country? Why, or why not?

Are there any conditions that might justify a person actively working against his or her country? If so, what are they?

Food for Thought

Courage can mean enduring intense pain for one's beliefs. But courage can also mean persisting through years of tedious or frustrating work. What kinds of courage do you need to complete the tasks God has for you? Notice the obstacles to discipleship that you encounter this week. As you do, ask yourself what kind of courage it will take to remain faithful to God in each situation. Then remember that you can find in God a never-ending supply of all the resources you will need.

You said, "Woe to me! The LORD has added
sorrow to my pain; I am worn out with groaning
and find no rest" (45:3).

— 10 —
No Rest for the Weary
Jeremiah 41–45

DIMENSION ONE:
WHAT DOES THE BIBLE SAY?

Answer these questions by reading Jeremiah 41

1. What crime does Ishmael commit? (41:2-8)

2. What does Ishmael do next? (41:10)

3. What happens to the captives at Gibeon? (41:11-14)

4. Why do the people not return to Mizpah? (41:17-18)

Answer these questions by reading Jeremiah 42

5. What do the people ask of Jeremiah? (42:1-3)

6. What promise do the people make? (42:5-6)

7. What is God's word for these people? (42:10-11, 19)

Answer these questions by reading Jeremiah 43

8. How do the people respond to Jeremiah's message? (43:1-3)
   They said Jeremiah was lying; God had not sent him to say not to go to Egypt rather Baruch was inciting Jeremiah against them in order to hand them over to the Babylonians

9. What do the people do? (43:5-7)
   They disobey the Lord's command to stay in the land of Judah and were led away by all the army officers

10. What happens to Jeremiah? (43:6-7)
    He was led away with all the men, women and children and in disobedience to the Lord entered Egypt.

11. What does Jeremiah do in Egypt, and what is the point of his demonstration? (43:8-11)
    Buried some large stones in clay in the brick pavement at the entrance to Pharaoh's palace at Tahpanhes. To declare what (how) he will set his "servant" Nebuchadnezzar's throne over the stones

Answer these questions by reading Jeremiah 44

12. Why has God destroyed the cities of Judah? (44:2-6)
    Because of all the evil they had done worshiping false gods

13. What question does God ask of the people? (44:7)
    "Why bring such great disaster on yourselves by cutting off from Judah the men and women, the children and infants and so leave yourselves without a remnant?"

14. How are the people bringing evil upon themselves?
(44:7-8) *By making idol gods; burning incense to other gods*

15. What does God intend to do? (44:12) *Take away the remnant of Judah who were determined to go to Egypt. They will all perish in Egypt (fall by the sword or die from famine).*

16. How do the people respond to this word from God?
(44:16-17)
They refused to listen and said they would continue to do as they had done

17. What other explanation do the people give for Judah's destruction? (44:18)
That ever since they had "stopped burning incense to the Queen of Heaven and pouring out drink offerings to her they have nothing and have been perishing by sword & famine.

18. What do the women say about their actions? (44:19)
(Read from bible).

Answer these questions by reading Jeremiah 45

19. When does Jeremiah offer this warning to Baruch?
(45:1-2) *In the 4th year of Jehoiakim son of Josiah king of Judah*

20. What troubles Baruch? (45:3)

21. Why should Baruch not seek great things for himself?
(45:4-5)

;

22. What promise does God give Baruch? (45:5)

DIMENSION TWO:
WHAT DOES THE BIBLE MEAN?

Jerusalem had fallen. The divinely protected capital lay in ashes. Most of the people were exiles in a distant land. Jeremiah had gone to live in Mizpah under the care of Gedaliah, whom the Babylonians had appointed governor. The prophet was now an old man. He had endured great pain. He had seen his most terrible prophecies fulfilled. Still, the worst was over. Perhaps now he could put together his own life and live out his days in relative peace. But no. Chapters 41–45 show us a very different ending to Jeremiah's unhappy life.

❑ *Jeremiah 41–43.* The war was over, but there was not yet peace in Judah. In these chapters we learn of several postwar events that involved Jeremiah in further conflict, unhappiness, and danger.

❑ *Jeremiah 41:1.* This is the man Johanan warned Gedaliah about (Jeremiah 40:13-14). Ishmael was captain of a field force and seems to have been among those who continued in guerrilla warfare even after the Babylonian victory. Both Johanan's charge and Ishmael's own later actions suggest that he was in league with Baalis, king of Ammon.

❑ *Jeremiah 41:2.* Gedaliah's trusting nature sealed his doom. He refused to believe Johanan's report and never guessed that Ishmael would stoop so low as to take advantage of a well-intentioned, perhaps conciliatory, dinner invitation. Gedaliah had hoped to smooth things over, to establish order and peace. Instead, he was killed; and the land was thrown into chaos once more.

❑ *Jeremiah 41:4-10.* Ishmael's cruelty and seeming irrationality make him terrifying indeed. We do not know what motivated this murderous outrage. We only know that many innocent people suffered for whatever evil lay within him.

❏ *Jeremiah 41:12.* Gibeon was about six miles northwest of Jerusalem. It was not on any direct route between the supposed sites of Mizpah and Ammon. Possibly Ishmael was taking a circuitous route to throw off pursuers. Or perhaps he was so crazed that he was driving his forces and their captives onward with no coherent plan.

❏ *Jeremiah 41:17.* The meaning of "Geruth Kimham" is unclear, but many scholars accept Kimham's Inn as the most likely possibility.

❏ *Jeremiah 42:4-7.* Jeremiah did not try to satisfy these people with instant prophecy. Ironically, his caution may have given the people more time to form their own opinions, making them less likely to follow the prophet's painstakingly derived advice.

❏ *Jeremiah 42:10.* The word *grieved* does not here connote sorrow for a misdeed. The term suggests only that God is turning away from punishment, that he does not plan to continue it.

❏ *Jeremiah 43:1-3.* The people who asked for the word of God do not like what they have received. So they deny that Jeremiah's message is genuine.

❏ *Jeremiah 43:4-7.* If Jeremiah believed that God wanted the people to remain in Judah, he surely would not have set out for Egypt willingly. He and Baruch were probably taken there by force. So Jeremiah, against his will and against the will of the God whom he served, left Judah, never to return. And once again the folly of some had led everyone, even the most innocent, toward disaster.

Tahpanhes is a city on the eastern border of Egypt.

❏ *Jeremiah 43:9-10.* Perhaps these stones are the makings of a large pedestal. Whether that is true or not, Jeremiah's meaning is clear. The people cannot escape Nebuchadnezzar's (and God's) wrath by fleeing to Egypt.

❏ *Jeremiah 43:13.* The center for sun worship at Heliopolis featured several tall, four-sided, stone pillars called obelisks. Three of these obelisks have survived. One is still in Heliopolis, one is in London, and one is in New York's Central Park. Those in New York and London are called "Cleopatra's Needle."

❏ *Jeremiah 44.* This chapter continues the picture of Jeremiah's life in Egypt. In particular we learn of a controversy that developed between Jeremiah and his countrymen.

❏ *Jeremiah 44:2-19.* The Queen of Heaven, a Babylonian fertility goddess, had long been popular in Israel, especially among women. Her worship had been banned by Josiah's reform (around 622 B.C.) but obviously did not disappear.

The people's response to Jeremiah shows little respect for the prophet or for the God he represents. We do not know exactly how this dispute ended. Legend has it that an angry mob eventually stoned Jeremiah to death for his unwelcome words.

❏ *Jeremiah 45.* Chapter 45 recalls an early conversation between Jeremiah and Baruch. Here a personal prophetic word spoken at the outset of their careers becomes, in retrospect, a summary of what their lives have held. As such it forms a fitting conclusion to this biographical section of the Book of Jeremiah.

❏ *Jeremiah 45:5.* Baruch may have hoped that Jeremiah's preaching would turn the nation around. If so, the people would be saved. The prophet and his friend might then become respected, even honored, figures in the community. But Jeremiah knew that this would not be the case. There would be no prizes or honors for them. Instead, Baruch would be lucky to get away with his skin. That much, and that much only, would God assure him.

DIMENSION THREE:
WHAT DOES THE BIBLE MEAN TO ME?

Expectations! Gedaliah, the pilgrims, Baruch, and perhaps even Jeremiah himself all experienced some shattered expectations. And some wide contrasts in human character had a lot to do with the shattering of these expectations. So, in this discussion we will be talking about expectations. We will also be talking about what we can expect of human nature and what we can expect of life itself.

Jeremiah 41:1-8, 11-42; 42:1-6; 43:1-7; 44:15-19; 45:1-4
Human Nature: What Can You Expect?

Human beings are not just animals operating on instinct. They have minds and wills and can make ethical choices. Some humans use these powers in godly fashion, exemplifying the very finest in human character. Others do not. Let's examine first some of the heights that humans may attain. What noble qualities do you see portrayed in Jeremiah 41:1, 4-7, 11-12; 42:1-6; 45:1-5?

Now for the depths that human beings may attain. What negative qualities do you see reflected in Jeremiah 41:1-8; 43:1-7; 44:15-19?

✻ Do you believe humans are born naturally good, naturally evil, or neutral?

Jeremiah 41:1-8; 43:4-7
With Some People, You Can Only Expect the Worst

As Gedaliah, the eighty pilgrims, and Jeremiah himself illustrate, innocent people sometimes suffer because of others' foolish or evil natures. Can you list any modern examples of this kind of suffering? If so, share your ideas with the group. How do such incidents make you feel?

Can we possibly anticipate and prepare for evil behavior in others? Could such anticipation have any side effects on us or on other people? If so, what?

Being victimized by someone else's evil can be a devastating experience. How can one cope with such an experience and the anger it produces?

Jeremiah 43:4-7; 45
And If You Spend Your Life in Service . . . ?

What would you say to a young woman who approached you with a problem? Suppose this young woman has looked forward for years to serving overseas as a missionary. Now suddenly she has begun to realize that this decision will mean a modest income subject to the international exchange rate, isolation from intellectual and cultural centers, fewer travel opportunities than she had hoped for, the danger of being caught in political upheavals, and almost no chance to meet young men. When she returns to the U.S., she will have few friends here; even relatives will be practically strangers. So now she is questioning whether she should spend her life in the mission field.

Most of us look forward to retirement as a time of well-earned relaxation and enjoyment. But this certainly was not what Jeremiah and Baruch experienced. They were plagued to their deaths by problems they in no way deserved. Does that happen often today? What are some realistic expectations one might have for the retirement years?

Food for Thought

Are your expectations of life and of other people realistic? Do they take into account both the depths and the heights human beings can attain? Do they include the possibility of some surprises along the way? Think about these questions as you anticipate and plan in the days ahead. Then remember that, whatever happens, God is still God and you are still his beloved child.

Like a lion coming up from Jordan's thickets
to a rich pastureland,
I will chase Edom from its land in an instant
(49:19).

11

God Is in Charge Here
Jeremiah 46–49

DIMENSION ONE:
WHAT DOES THE BIBLE SAY?

Answer these questions by reading Jeremiah 46

1. What is the message of this chapter? (46:1)

2. What nation does the first passage concern? (46:2)

3. What incident has inspired this message? (46:2)

4. What preparations do the soldiers make for battle? (46:3-4)

5. What happens in the battle? (46:5)

6. What is Egypt's ambition? (46:8)

7. Whose day is the day of battle? (46:10)

8. What does Jeremiah prophesy God doing in the north country? (46:10)

9. What is the subject of the second message? (46:13)

10. Why do Egypt's warriors not stand? (46:15)

11. What will happen to the "Daughter of Egypt"? (46:24)

12. Why should Jacob not fear? (46:28)

Answer these questions by reading Jeremiah 47

13. What nation does this message concern? (47:1)

14. What does Jeremiah think will happen to the Philistines? (47:2)

15. What is the Lord doing? (47:4)

Answer these questions by reading Jeremiah 48

16. On what nation does this message focus? (48:1)

17. What is happening to Moab, and why? (48:3-4, 7)

18. What good fortune has Moab previously enjoyed? (48:11)

19. Of what sin is Moab guilty? (48:26, 29)

20. What hope does the prophet offer? (48:47)

Answer these questions by reading Jeremiah 49

21. Of what nations do the messages in this chapter speak? (49:1, 7, 23, 28, 34)

22. What is God about to do to these nations? (49:2, 14, 27, 28, 35-36)

23. To what animal does God liken himself? (49:19)

DIMENSION TWO:
WHAT DOES THE BIBLE MEAN?

The story of Jeremiah's life has been told. We have read collections of his public prophecies and heard his cries of personal anguish. Still, someone believed one more major group of messages belonged in the Book of Jeremiah. These are the prophecies against foreign nations. This collection is found in Jeremiah 46:1–51:58. Some of these prophecies are Jeremiah's. Some almost certainly were written by someone else. Some seem to relish the defeat of enemy lands. Others offer words of hope to those same peoples. But these are all prophetic words that someone cherished enough to preserve. They express a profound belief in God's power and in his sovereignty over every nation on earth. In this respect, at least, they all reflect a basic element of Jeremiah's faith.

❏ *Jeremiah 46.* Here we find prophecies of Egypt's destruction. They are very likely Jeremiah's own. The prose comment and words of comfort for Israel that conclude the chapter, however, are probably later additions.

❏ *Jeremiah 46:2.* The event that inspired this poem was the battle of Carchemish (605 B.C.). With this battle Nebuchadnezzar decisively defeated Egypt and established Babylonia's dominance over the entire Middle East.

❏ *Jeremiah 46:9.* The name *Put* probably refers to an area along the eastern coast of Africa. Lydia, or Lud, was also in Africa. These peoples were apparently allied with Egypt.

❏ *Jeremiah 46:10.* Going into battle, the warriors naturally wonder who will win the day. The day, however, belongs to

God alone. His is the power that will out. But "day of the Lord" carries an additional meaning. The day of the Lord is the day of universal judgment.

❑ *Jeremiah 46:14.* Migdol, Memphis, and Tahpanhes were all cities in Egypt.

❑ *Jeremiah 46:18.* Tabor and Carmel are mountains. Thus Jeremiah suggests that Babylonia towers over Egypt.

❑ *Jeremiah 46:19-24.* Here Jeremiah uses a variety of images, including a heifer, a snake, and a human daughter, to portray Egypt's powerlessness against Babylonian might. Nebuchadnezzar did, in fact, invade Egypt in 568 B.C.; but he never succeeded in actually conquering it.

❑ *Jeremiah 46:25.* Amon was a god especially associated with Thebes, the capital of Upper Egypt.

❑ *Jeremiah 47–49.* These chapters contain messages directed toward many more of Israel's neighbors. In both plain words and striking imagery, we learn that these nations too must bear the force of God's wrath.

❑ *Jeremiah 47:4.* Tyre and Sidon were Phoenician, not Philistine, cities. However, it is possible that the two nations were allied at the time.

Caphtor is another name for Crete.

❑ *Jeremiah 47:5-7.* Gaza and Ashkelon were major Philistine cities. The Anakim were a tribe of giants that Joshua all but wiped out in his conquest of the Promised Land. According to Joshua 11:21-22, he left only a few Anakim living in the Philistine cities of Gaza, Gath, and Ashdod.

Cutting oneself and shaving the head were signs of mourning.

❑ *Jeremiah 48:1-6.* These verses and others in Chapter 48 contain a number of place names. All these places were in Moab, except perhaps Heshbon. The meaning of the word translated "Madmen" is unknown. The context, however, suggests that it was a Moabite city or tribe.

❑ *Jeremiah 48:7.* Chemosh was the Moabite god.

❑ *Jeremiah 48:8.* The valley is that of the lower Jordan, on the east side of the river north of the Dead Sea.

❑ *Jeremiah 48:11.* With a mountainous terrain, a secluded location, and a little adroit politicking, Moab has escaped the winds of war more successfully than Israel has. The writer augments this picture of Moab's protected position by comparing the country to undisturbed bottles of wine.

❑ *Jeremiah 48:12.* This verse continues the wine bottle image. Now, though, someone is coming to tilt those bottles, to spill out the wine, to destroy the vessels. To Moab, too, the wrath of God will come.

❑ *Jeremiah 48:13.* Bethel was the name of a sanctuary city in northern Israel, but it was also the name of a deity. This god was worshiped by the Syrians and by some Jews living in Egypt. We cannot be sure whether this verse refers to the city or to the god.

❑ *Jeremiah 48:45.* Sihon was an ancient Amorite king whose capital was Heshbon. After his defeat, Israel and Moab frequently fought over control of his city.

❑ *Jeremiah 49:1.* The Israelite tribe of Gad had originally settled in the territory east of the Jordan. In 732 B.C., however, the Syrians conquered the area and took its people into exile. Thereupon the Amorites (with their god Milcom) moved in. The prophet here insists that they had no right to do so.

❑ *Jeremiah 49:2-3.* Rabbah is the modern-day Ammon, capital of Jordan.

Heshbon changed hands frequently. It was apparently under Ammonite control at the time of this prophecy.

Ai was a city in northern Israel, but it seems unlikely that Ai is the place referred to here. No second Ai is known, however.

❑ *Jeremiah 49:7-8.* Teman and Dedan were districts in Edom. Israel's brother, Esau, was the legendary ancestor of the Edomites.

❑ *Jeremiah 49:13.* Bozrah was Edom's chief city.

❑ *Jeremiah 49:23.* Damascus was the capital of Syria. Hamath and Arpad were Syrian cities. Since all these cities lost independent existence before 732 B.C., some scholars assume that this prophecy is a very old one. Others, however, believe that it is a product of the post-exilic period deliberately "antiqued" to seem like ancient writ.

❑ *Jeremiah 49:27.* The name *Ben-Hadad* was shared by several kings of Damascus.

❑ *Jeremiah 49:28.* Kedar and Hazor were semi-nomadic Arabian tribes that inhabited desert areas on the fringes of Palestine.

❑ *Jeremiah 49:32.* "In distant places" can also be translated as "Cutting the corners of the hair," which was part of an Arabian religious rite.

❑ *Jeremiah 49:34-39.* Elam was a country east of Babylon and north of the Persian Gulf. It is the only nation addressed in this group of messages that was not a fairly close neighbor of Israel. "Early in the reign of Zedekiah" dates the prophecy to 598 B.C. or early 597 B.C. However, we know so little of Elamite history during this period that we have no clue as to what circumstances might have elicited these words.

DIMENSION THREE: WHAT DOES THE BIBLE MEAN TO ME?

God is an awesome power. God can destroy any nation on earth. That is what the passages of Scripture for this session have been telling us. But what place does that message have in the modern world? Does it mean anything for us, for our decisions, for our country's international relations? The questions below should help you consider some possibilities.

Jeremiah 47:2-3, 6-7; 48:40; 49:19, 36
Imagine the Power!

The poetic prophecies for this session contain several colorful, but ancient, images of destructive power. What expresses the idea of a powerful force to the modern mind? To find out, try completing the following poetic fragment several times, using only modern words and terms:

Like a _____ will the Lord come upon you.

With _____ he will strike,
    and you will know both terror and destruction.

Now take a closer look at the words you have used to fill in the blanks. Could God actually use any of the forces you have mentioned to punish or destroy a modern nation? Do you believe God would do something like this?

Jeremiah 48:7, 29-31, 42; 49:1-2
National Decisions and God's Demands

Do you believe that God expects modern nations to obey his laws in national and international decision making? How would obeying God's laws be reflected in national policy?

What policies or attitudes of modern nations stand in disobedience to God? Are these concepts different from the sins that destroyed Moab and Ammon? If so, how would you describe these differences?

Jeremiah 48:1, 7-8, 14-17; 49:16, 19, 27, 35; see also
Jeremiah 3:21-23; 4:1-2; 17:12-13; 25:4-6
A Question of Defense

You may also want to read Jeremiah 3:21-23; 4:1-2; 17:12-13; 25:4-6 before you consider these questions. Our times have seen much debate over which missile, which bomb, or which plane will offer us the best defense. The passages of Scripture above, however, suggest that military preparations are not a foolproof method of security. If they are not able to secure our national defense, what is? Does the Bible imply that there is another, more reliable, source of security? If so, what is that source of security? How would you design a national defense strategy based upon this biblical idea of security?

We have had this wisdom available since ancient times. Why, then, do so few national defense plans seem to incorporate the biblical idea of security?

Jeremiah 46:2; 47:1; 48:1; 49:1, 7, 23, 28, 34
What Would You Say?

If you could send a letter based on this session's study to any national leader on earth, to whom would you write and what would you say?

Food for Thought

Where are earth's nations headed, and what are you doing to influence their direction? Think seriously about these questions this week. Then choose one specific action that you will carry through in response.

GOD IS IN CHARGE HERE

93

The people of Israel are oppressed,
and the people of Judah as well (50:33).

—— 12 ——

What Does It All Mean?

Jeremiah 50–52

DIMENSION ONE:
WHAT DOES THE BIBLE SAY?

Answer these questions by reading Jeremiah 50

1. What nation is the subject of these prophecies? (50:1)

   Babylon.

2. What news does God give his prophet to proclaim? (50:2)

   That Babylon is taken, Bel is confounded, Merodach is broken in pieces, her idols confounded, her images broken in pieces.

3. With what attitude do the people come seeking the Lord? (50:4)

4. With what purpose do the people turn toward Zion? (50:5)

5. How does Jeremiah describe the people? (50:6)

6. Why can enemies claim guiltlessness in devouring these people? (50:7)

7. Why is Babylon falling? (50:15)

8. How does Jeremiah describe Israel? (50:17)

9. What has Nebuchadnezzar done, and what is God doing to him in return? (50:17-18)

10. What promises does God make to Israel? (50:19-20)

11. What does this writer expect the people to do when they reach Zion? (50:28)

12. Why should the archers come against Babylon? (50:29)

13. What suffering afflicts God's people, and what hope do they see? (50:33-34)

Answer these questions by reading Jeremiah 51

14. What would the Jews have done for Babylon if they could? (51:9)

15. What meaning does Babylon's fall hold for the Jews? (51:10)

16. What is the difference between Israel's God and the idols? (51:17-19)

17. Upon whom should Jerusalem's blood be? (51:35)

18. What advice does the prophet offer for these times of violence and political upheaval? (51:45-46)

19. How might the universe respond to Babylon's destruction? (51:47-48)

20. What does Jeremiah command Seraiah to do? (51:61-64)

21. What has God done to Jerusalem and Judah, and why? (52:3)

DIMENSION TWO:
WHAT DOES THE BIBLE MEAN?

Torn from their homes and possessions by a devastating war, thousands of Jews had been herded off to live in an enemy land. They were depressed by their political and material losses. But more than that, they were oppressed by a staggering blow to their religious faith. They were God's chosen people! They had counted on God's eternal protection. And now this! What could it mean? And where could they go from here?

Through long years of exile the Jews struggled to answer those questions. Here, in these concluding chapters of the Book of Jeremiah, we find some of the results of that struggle. This section is a collection of writings by many unnamed prophets. Some of these writings date from the beginning of the Exile, some from nearer the end. These writers do not all approach their problem from the same perspective, nor do they all draw the same conclusions. But each is trying to meet the need for some understanding of the traumatic past, the pain-filled present, and the uncertain future.

❏ *Jeremiah 50.* Why is Israel defeated and in exile? Some of the prophecies we find in this chapter insist that God's people are victims of Babylonian evil, others that this is God's punishment for Israel's own sin. Then what does the future hold? Some of the writers look forward mostly to Babylon's destruction as vindication for Israel's suffering. Others look toward their people's own repentance and God's forgiveness. But they all hope for Israel's eventual return to the Promised Land.

❏ *Jeremiah 50:2.* The names *Marduk* (NIV) and *Merodach* (NRSV) both refer to the chief Babylonian god. Bel is a title that denotes supremacy. Thus Bel also refers to Marduk.

WHAT DOES IT ALL MEAN? **97**

❑ *Jeremiah 50:3.* Babylon fell to the Persians in 539 B.C., many years after Nebuchadnezzar's conquest of Jerusalem.

❑ *Jeremiah 50:5.* Covenant renewal, not vengeance, is the goal here.

❑ *Jeremiah 50:21.* The name of a region in southern Babylonia has here been altered to Merathaim, which means double rebellion or double bitterness. The word *Pekod*, which means punishment, plays on the name of a tribe from eastern Babylonia.

❑ *Jeremiah 50:23.* Babylon is here pictured as a hammer that has been smashing the whole earth but is now "broken and shattered" itself.

❑ *Jeremiah 50:28.* For this writer, the high point of Israel's return to Zion would be the declaration of vengeance.

❑ *Jeremiah 51.* The collection of exilic prophecies continues through most of this chapter. The final six verses, however, relate an incident dated during Zedekiah's reign, before the fall of Jerusalem.

❑ *Jeremiah 51:9.* Note here the very different tone of concern for Babylon.

❑ *Jeremiah 51:11.* The Medes inhabited the highlands east of Babylonia. Around 560 B.C. many expected these Medes to attack the empire, but that attack never came.

❑ *Jeremiah 51:20-23.* The prophet never specifies who this "war club" is. Perhaps this was originally part of a longer poem addressed to an enemy of Babylonia. Or, it could have been addressed to Babylonia itself by a poet who shared Jeremiah's viewpoint.

❑ *Jeremiah 51:27-33.* Ararat, Minni, and Ashkenaz refer to peoples living north of Babylon. They had been conquered by the Medes and are now summoned to help the Medes attack Babylon. The entire poem is a vivid picture of hoped-for destruction. Actually, when Babylon did fall to the Persians, it surrendered peacefully and intact.

❑ *Jeremiah 51:35.* "May our blood be on . . ." casts upon the Babylonians the guilt for shedding blood.

❑ *Jeremiah 51:59-64.* This appendix seems to have been added by the editor of this material to show that all these prophecies follow the thinking of Jeremiah. Scholars, however, disagree strongly over whether the incident is historically accurate.

❑ *Jeremiah 52.* This final chapter is a detailed historical account of the fall of Jerusalem. We read this same story in Jeremiah 39. The version found in this chapter contains the addition of more detail, some brief commentary, and a postscript on Jehoiachin's fate.

❑ *Jeremiah 52:2-3.* Here the writer offers his explanation of the Jerusalem tragedy. Like Jeremiah, he sees the event as punishment for Judah's sin.

❑ *Jeremiah 52:31.* The thirty-seventh year of Jehoiachin's exile was 561 B.C.

Evil-Merodach is a misspelling of Amel-Marduk, son of Nebuchadnezzar. The variant spelling may have been intentional as it makes the name mean stupid person.

DIMENSION THREE:
WHAT DOES THE BIBLE MEAN TO ME?

During and after any major event, people who take life and religion at all seriously usually do some tall thinking. They ponder the meaning of what has happened, reevaluate their part in it, search for lessons they might learn, and think through the event's implications for their future life and faith. As they do so, all the persons involved may not reach the same conclusions. That is what happened to the exiled Jews in the sixth century B.C. But it could also be happening in your nation or in your church right now. Use the questions below to help you think about this whole process of trying to find meaning in the events we experience.

Jeremiah 50:6-7, 17-20, 33-34; 52:35; 52:3
Reflecting on the Process of Reflection

Why do you think people, whether ancient Jews or modern Americans, do so much reflecting upon past and present events? Does this process fill a need? Does the process serve some practical purpose?

Can you think of any past or current events that we as a nation are still trying to interpret—events upon which people continue to disagree? If so, what are those events?

As a religious person, what is your starting point for interpreting events? Is this starting point different from that of others in our society? Could it lead you to different conclusions from those your neighbor reaches?

If Christians begin from the same basic starting point in discussing a particular issue, why do they not all reach the same conclusions? If you agree that this is the case, give examples of this problem.

Jeremiah 1–52
Pondering Our Own Recent Experiences

We hope that this study of the Book of Jeremiah has proved an important experience to you individually and as a group. If it has, then perhaps some reflection on the study is appropriate at this time.

What were your impressions of the book as a whole? Share your thoughts with the group.

Do you think this book has any particular meaning or message for our world today? If so, what?

Has anything in the book's message especially influenced your personal thinking or actions?

Has Jeremiah as a person had any special impact upon your life? If so, what?

Food for Thought

What do you do with the important events in your personal or community life? Do they just happen and then pass away all unnoticed? Or do you do some serious thinking about these events? If you do reflect upon them, is God the basis and focus of that thinking? Do you try to understand what is happening from his viewpoint? Does your faith in God free you to look at things in new or unusual ways? Can you recognize that others' opinions may differ from yours? Spend some time thinking about your patterns of reflection. Then consider some ways you might make that reflection more frequent, more open, and more God centered than it already is.

Arise, cry out in the night . . .
pour out your heart like water
in the presence of the Lord (2:19).

— 13 —
Cry Out to the Lord
Lamentations 1–5

DIMENSION ONE:
WHAT DOES THE BIBLE SAY?

Answer these questions by reading Lamentations 1

1. The poem opens by contrasting the city's past with its present. What are the differences? (1:1)

2. How have the city's friends responded? (1:2)

3. Why do the roads to Zion mourn? (1:4)

4. Why have foes overtaken the city? (1:5)

5. What cry does Jerusalem raise to her onlookers? (1:12)

6. What has God fashioned from Jerusalem's sins? (1:14)

Answer these questions by reading Lamentations 2

7. What has the Lord become for Israel? (2:5)

8. What has God done to the place of meeting? (2:6-7)

9. What is happening to Jerusalem's children? (2:11-12)

10. What fault does the poet find in Judah's prophets? (2:14)

11. What does the poet call upon his people to do? (2:18-19)

Answer these questions by reading Lamentations 3

12. As this poem opens, who is speaking? (3:1)

13. What thought gives the poet hope? (3:21-23)

14. How should one respond to the Lord's yoke? (3:28-30)

15. Is the Lord cruel and merciless? (3:31-33)

16. Where do both calamities and good things come from? (3:38)

17. What course of action does the poem recommend? (3:40-42)

18. What has God done for the afflicted? (3:57-58)

Answer these questions by reading Lamentations 4

19. What belief has proved sadly mistaken? (4:12)

20. What comfort does the poet derive as he thinks of Edom? (4:22)

Answer these questions by reading Lamentations 5

21. What does the poet ask of God? (5:1)

22. What final plea does the poet make? (5:21)

23. With what possibility does this prayer end? (5:22)

DIMENSION TWO:
WHAT DOES THE BIBLE MEAN?

The Book of Lamentations is, as its name implies, a book of grief. Its five poems cry out from the depths of suffering, yet they reveal a faith that is deeper still. With few exceptions, scholars recognize these as songs composed for public mourning after Jerusalem's destruction in 587 B.C. Filled with eyewitness details, these poems outline both the horrors and the questions that arose with the siege and its aftermath. And this is surely one of the poet's (or poets') purposes. The poet wanted to help the people face their terrible pain. But this book is no mere catalogue of misery. The book is the excruciating effort of one or more sensitive, thinking individuals to explain why this suffering has come about and what it means for Israel's relationship with God. These poems recount the pain. They also reveal the sin that caused the pain. But most of all they form, from the midst of desolation, an offering of faith and hope.

The New International Version and the New Revised Standard Version entitle this book *Lamentations*. The title itself is somewhat later than the book's content. Hebrew manuscripts call the collection simply *How*, from its opening word. The traditional assumption that Jeremiah wrote the poems is a later one. Few scholars today defend that assumption. Differences in style, language, and thought make it very unlikely that the prophet Jeremiah could have composed them.

Each of these poems has twenty-two verses (or a multiple thereof), one (or more) for each letter of the Hebrew alphabet. The rhythms are those commonly found in funeral or grief songs.

❏ *Lamentations 1:1.* This opening verse sets the book's tone of sorrow and grief. Three times the poet compares Jerusalem's former glory with her present devastation and servitude. The second figure in the series, that of a widow, stresses the city's vulnerable position. In Hebrew society, widows and orphans were the most defenseless persons.

❑ *Lamentations 1:3.* At the time this poem was written, most of Judah's citizens had gone as captives to Babylon. (Note numerous references to the city's emptiness throughout these poems.)

❑ *Lamentations 1:10.* The Babylonians also took many of the Temple treasures. You may recall the extensive listing of such items in Jeremiah 52:17-23.

❑ *Lamentations 1:11.* This and other descriptive statements point to a critical lack of food in the city.

❑ *Lamentations 1:15.* The term *Virgin Daughter* emphasizes Judah's helplessness and the shame and tragedy of her despoiling. The image of the winepress stresses the brutality and completeness of her destruction.

❑ *Lamentations 2:1.* God's "footstool" would be Zion or the Temple.

❑ *Lamentations 2:4.* "All who were pleasing to the eye" refers to the bright young men, the talented and responsible leaders who all showed ability or promise.

❑ *Lamentations 2:6.* Here the poet characterizes the Temple as a flimsy booth, a temporary shelter used in a garden or field.

❑ *Lamentations 2:9.* Here, as in many other spots, lurks the fear that God has indeed abandoned his people.

❑ *Lamentations 2:20.* The famine had apparently grown so severe that instances of cannibalism occurred.

❑ *Lamentations 3:15, 19.* Gall is also a bitter herb (The NRSV mentions "wormwood."), symbolizing the bitterness of Judah's experience.

❑ *Lamentations 3:22-24.* Here, in the midst of desolation and grief, we find one of the most profound statements of faith ever recorded.

❑ *Lamentations 3:28-30.* The writer counsels patient acceptance of suffering.

❑ *Lamentations 3:31-36.* The poet acknowledges that all this suffering comes from God. Yet he maintains his faith in the Lord's never-ending love.

❑ *Lamentations 3:63.* "Sitting or standing" is a picturesque way of saying "at leisure and at work" or "from morning 'til night."

❏ *Lamentations 4:1-2.* A startling, horrible thing has happened! That which is intrinsically valuable has been treated as junk!

❏ *Lamentations 4:3.* The female ostrich was believed to be quite neglectful of her young.

❏ *Lamentations 4:5.* Purple was the color of royalty.

❏ *Lamentations 4:19.* Some have seen this verse to be evidence that the poet was with Zedekiah and the others who tried to escape Nebuchadnezzar's army.

❏ *Lamentations 4:21-22.* Edom had participated in the original plot to rebel against Babylon. Later, however, she turned and joined the Babylonians in capturing Jerusalem. Soon thereafter, groups of Edomites moved into depopulated portions of southern Judah. Naturally, the people of Judah viewed their treacherous neighbor with special bitterness. They relished the thought that she too would someday reap her well-deserved punishment.

❏ *Lamentations 5:6.* "Submitted to" is translated from a phrase that literally means to shake hands on a deal or to pay homage to. In Judah's position, any deal could only be a sellout.

❏ *Lamentations 5:8.* "Slaves" is a slurring reference to the Jewish and/or Babylonian underlings who are now administering the nation.

❏ *Lamentations 5:9.* Going outside the city walls to find food could be very dangerous, as bands of Bedouin tribesmen and other unruly characters roamed the uninhabited land.

❏ *Lamentations 5:19-22.* Here the awful fear that God has abandoned his people erupts explicitly. The people face the possibility and pray that God will not let this be so.

DIMENSION THREE:
WHAT DOES THE BIBLE MEAN TO ME?

All life involves pain. Some lives include pain in a devastating degree. In the Book of Lamentations we have felt the sufferings, the questions, the struggles for faith and hope of a totally beaten people. Their cries tug at our hearts because we too have suffered, and we know that we may well suffer again. Let's use this discussion time, then, to think a bit about those times of pain, the questions and fears they raise, and the kind of faith that can withstand them.

Lamentations 1:1, 10-11; 2:11-12, 20-21; 3:1-6
Such Terrible Suffering!

Famine, disease, sudden or lingering death in a city reduced to rubble—these were the lot of those who remained after the fall of Jerusalem. Today we see such things on television newscasts. But could we here in the United States ever experience this kind of suffering? What events could cause it?

Even in times of national tranquillity we experience many personally painful events. What are some of these events?

What Will We Do With This Pain?

Elisabeth Kübler-Ross and others have identified several basic components of the grieving process. These include denial, anger, bargaining, depression, and acceptance. Within these components lie some common attitudes and behaviors. These behaviors include a withdrawal from family and friends, the questioning "Why me?", laying the blame on others, regret (if only we had done such-and-such), and concern over real or imagined guilt. Most people go through all these reactions whenever they experience any significant loss. You can find many of these components in Lamentations 1:12; 2:10, 20; 3:25-33, 37-39, 59-66; 4:12-13; 5-7, 16, 19-22. Identify in these passages as many grief factors as you can.

Can you imagine yourself experiencing any of these grief reactions?

Lamentations 2:18-19; 3:21-24, 26-33, 40-41 suggest several actions we can take in dealing with our pain. What are these actions? Do you think they would be helpful? Would they be easy to carry out?

Lamentations 3:1-3, 21-33—Hope? In What?

How can anyone hope in God at such a time, especially if one suspects that God himself has caused the suffering?

Lamentations 1–5
What Do the Lamentations Say to You?

If you were experiencing a great deal of sorrow or pain, do you think you would find the poems in Lamentations helpful? Or would they add to your distress?

Is there any passage in Lamentations that has held special meaning for you? If so, which one?

Food for Thought

Everyone suffers. Everyone grieves. The writer(s) of Lamentations did, and so do we all. Take note this week of the expressions of pain and grief you encounter. Then ask yourself where your God fits into situations like these.